Commercial Real Estate Career Education and Resource Guide

The Hoyt Institute of Real Estate

Sponsored by:

Appraisal Institute®
Professionals Providing Real Estate Solutions

CCIM

COSTAR GROUP

naiop
National Association of Industrial and Office Properties
Building Better Communities
NAIOP RESEARCH FOUNDATION

PREA
pension real estate association

Commercial Real Estate
Career Education and Resource Guide

The Hoyt Institute of Real Estate (HIRE)
Tel: 561-694-7621 email at weimer@hoyt.org
Web site at www.hoyt.org
The Homer Hoyt Center
760 US Highway One, Suite 300
North Palm Beach, FL 33408

Written by:
Norm Miller, Ph.D. University of Cincinnati
normmiller@fuse.net

Margot Weinstein, Ph.D.
drmargot@drmargotweinstein.com

Edited by:
Alison Sampson, MA, University of Cincinnati
Alison.sampson@uc.edu

William Sikes, MA, University of Cincinnati
William.sikes@uc.edu

with assistance from Jeff Fisher, Ph.D., Indiana University

International Standard Book Number 0-9776579-0-6

Printed in the United States of America

Dedication:

This resource guide is dedicated to Dr. Maury Seldin, Founder of the Homer Hoyt Institute, the Hoyt Institute of Real Estate and the Weimer School, the only Post-Doc real estate school in the world.

Acknowledgements:

This resource is the result of discussions at the Homer Hoyt Institute, ARES (American Real Estate Society) and NAIOP (National Association of Industrial and Office Properties) meetings. Jim Delisle, Geoff Dohrmann, Maury Seldin, Larry Wofford, Roy Black, Stephen Roulac, Susanne Cannon, Kerry Vandell, Jeff Fisher, Wayne Tiedge, Arthur Adler, Marshall Bennett, Gerald W. Fogelson, E. Rene Frank, Steven L. Good, Daniel L. Goodwin, Peter Linneman, Dale Anne Reiss, David Simon, Nancy Suvarnamani, Ruth Theobald, Sam Zell, Steve Felix, and many others have contributed to the undertaking of this resource guide.

Many thanks to our sponsors:

Appraisal Institute, CCIM, CoStar, NAIOP Research Foundation, and PREA

Commercial Real Estate Career Education and Resource Guide

Table of Contents

Info on Ordering More Copies of This Resource can be found on the back cover of this book.

Why a Resource Guide for Commercial Real Estate?

Commercial real estate provides many exciting career opportunities. Unfortunately not everyone knows about these opportunities. Here we provide a resource to better understand the professional paths that someone in this industry might follow. High school students, university students, and career counselors may benefit by knowing more about the various career opportunities in appraisal, brokerage, leasing, corporate real estate, development, real estate finance, real estate law, institutional investment, property management, consulting and planning and more. We also wanted to provide a resource for those who want to expand or continue their professional education through the leading trade associations as well as graduate programs in real estate. Organizations like CCIM (Certified Commercial Investment Member Institute), the National Association of Industrial and Office Properties (NAIOP), the Appraisal Institute (AI), the Pension Real Estate Association (PREA), and others provide conferences that cover important industry trends as well as seminars and professional designations. Many of these are cutting edge and highly respected designations. As the speed of economic transformation accelerates, our knowledge continually needs to be updated and this is where the trade associations are critical for continued professional advancement.

Much of the material in Part 1 has been extracted from "Real Estate Principles in the New Economy" by Norm Miller and David Geltner, with permission from Thompson Southwestern Publishers, 2005.

Part 1

Introduction to Commercial Real Estate Careers and Paths to Success

Introduction to Commercial Real Estate Careers and Paths to Success

Real estate involves virtually every field of business and many outside of business. That is why we find it so exciting! In fact, it is one of the best areas to study for general business background simply because real estate problems and cases require the integration of many different disciplines.

Is Real Estate a Discipline?

Academics seem to take delight in this debate. Professors who teach "real estate" usually have training in finance, economics and a variety of other business skills. This sort of "existentialistic debate" on whether real estate is a discipline unto itself is founded in a search for the justification of the study of real estate as a key curriculum component of a complete business education. But the enormous proportion of business and personal wealth tied up in real estate is reason enough to study real estate, whether or not it is a unique discipline as opposed to an applied field. Real estate programs that offer two year degrees, four year degrees, MBAs as well as other Masters programs now exist at hundreds of colleges around the United States and Canada. Real estate programs also exist in the United Kingdom under the name of "surveying" or "real property" and in the Netherlands, Singapore, Hong Kong, France, Canada, Germany and others. Three of the largest programs in the world exist in Singapore at the National University of Singapore, NUS, in Germany at the European Business School and in England at Reading University. Real estate programs are now emerging in many of the newly industrialized nations like Thailand, South Korea, China, and Russia. In fact, real estate skills including valuation methodologies which feed into development, financing, and investment decisions are essential in order to develop efficient capital markets.

A separate discipline requires relationship principles (core knowledge) that are unique to it alone, such as those found in physics and math. Few business fields will purely meet such a test, but enough knowledge has been produced within areas like finance that most people will view this as a "discipline". But whether there are unique relationships that apply only to real estate does not really matter. Real estate is such a vital component of any modern economy and so important in the standard of living that most of us desire, that there is no question that the study of real estate is worth your time.

Real Estate Skills, Self-Assessment and Careers Paths

What are the required skills and career opportunities available in the real estate industry? Real estate professionals must be able to research, analyze, negotiate, plan, market, manage and often work long days. Before going into detail on skills and career paths, first think about the question: "What am I good at?" A good place to start before thinking about any career is with an honest self-assessment. Imagine a straight line axis with two extreme personality attributes at opposite ends: "analytical" versus "people-oriented."

Pure Analytical Type	⟵⟶	Pure People Type

Very few of us are both highly analytical and highly people-oriented, but rather fall somewhere in between. Analytical types are comfortable with research and quantitative analysis, enjoy learning new technical skills, and like problem modeling and solving. People oriented types are extroverts by nature who prefer working with people, talking and socializing as opposed to sitting behind a computer.

Certain real estate specializations tend to require more of the analytical attribute while others require more of the people-oriented attribute. For example, appraisers, mortgage lenders, corporate real estate managers and property managers must be strong on the analytical side with strong written skills. Brokers and leasing agents require strong interpersonal, negotiation, and verbal skills. Developers, commercial mortgage brokers, and real estate consultants must have a heavy dose of both.

What do Real Estate People Need to Know?

Real estate people can never know too much. They must constantly strive to stay abreast of business trends, and think about issues affecting their clients, businesses and investments such as current tax laws, new highway routes or new modes of transportation, technological trends, interest rate trends, or the implications of existing and proposed zoning regulations. Beyond a general knowledge of business and economics, employers expect neophyte real estate professionals to be computer and communication system literate with spreadsheets, data base analysis, word processing, graphical analysis and geographic information systems. They also expect new employees to communicate well and to be able to make oral presentations. Negotiation skills are also an important aspect of the real estate industry, and students should practice these while in school. Specific career paths are discussed below along with key trade associations.

All of the trade associations listed in the sections below can be found using links from https://www.business.uc.edu/realestate/trade

Appraisal and Consulting

Appraisers are paid to estimate the value of property after a systematic analysis of the prices of similar properties or based on an analysis of discounted future cash flows derived from an estimate of rents less operating expenses and financing. This valuation estimate requires an analysis of the market and the subject property being appraised. Most appraisers work for a variety of clients on a per assignment fee basis, while others are internal staff appraisers producing value opinions for their employer. Most appraisers specialize in residential property or specific types of commercial property. Federal laws in the U.S. require that any appraisal required when the government is involved directly or indirectly must be done by a state certified appraiser. Certification is at two levels, residential and general, and is based on a combination of tests and experience. Trade association designations require more experience and education than the state certification process and also are required by many clients, the most respected of which for commercial property is the MAI for Member of the Appraisal Institute. A similar group with broader exposure in Asia and Europe is the Royal Institute of Chartered Surveyors or RICS.

The outlook for appraisers involved in specialized commercial appraisal and consulting, such as site analysis, buy versus lease decisions, property tax appeals, portfolio re-valuation, and investment analysis is quite promising. Many commercial and consulting oriented appraisers work within larger consulting firms including accounting and market research firms.

Technology is having a major impact on the commercial and residential sectors of the real estate industry. The outlook for residential appraisal is being greatly influenced by the introduction of new technology and automated appraisal techniques. Opportunities abound for real estate professionals to revolutionize the automation of the residential sector, and at the same time, residential appraisal firms that do not embrace the new technology may become extinct.

For more information about appraisal and consulting see the trade associations, the Appraisal Institute under **AI**, the Royal Institute of Chartered Surveyors under RICS and the Real Estate Counselors under CRE listed at the trade association web site.

Brokerage and Leasing

Real estate agents that represent buyers, sellers, owners or tenants must be licensed by the states in which they work. All states require a test before issuing a sales license. The more advanced broker's license requires more experience and education as well as an additional license test provided at the state level. Some states allow reciprocity where a license in one state satisfies for an application to do business in another state.

The public perception of the real estate industry is often based on images of residential sales agents, since this is the most visible and highly advertised segment of the real estate industry. Residential agents represent buyers or sellers in exchange for a fee, which is generally only payable based on the completion of a sale known as a contingency fee. This productivity-based segment of the industry requires long and uncertain hours, often resulting in the vast majority of sales agents dropping out of the industry because their commissions provide inadequate financial support. Those that succeed can make very attractive incomes. People skills dominate this field, and a lack of college education has not hindered many successful residential agents. The current outlook for residential brokers and agents is positive for those involved in the utilization of the available internet and intranet technology for marketing and efficiently working with buyers and sellers.

Continuing education is generally required by the licensing authorities in each state and many agents take advantage of programs offered by the National Association of Realtors or

NAR at the national, state or local level.

Commercial brokerage requires both people skills and a much higher level of technical business knowledge. For this reason most successful commercial agents need at least an undergraduate education and many have graduate degrees in business, enabling them to work with corporations, tenants, institutional buyers and sellers, domestic and foreign business entities and a host of sophisticated investment and business clients. Within the commercial industry most agents specialize in a particular type of property such as industrial, office, retail, hotels, apartments, recreational and parking. Most commercial agents are constantly involved in continuing education activities through a variety of trade associations. Successful commercial agents earn executive level compensation or more but must watch the markets closely to anticipate economic trends affecting the real estate industry.

For opportunities in commercial brokerage and leasing see CCIM**,** Certified Commercial Investment Member**,** SIOR, Society of Industrial and Office REALTORS, NAIOP**,** National Association of Industrial and Office Properties, CoreNet, Corporate Real Estate Network, ICSC, International Council of Shopping Centers, and CREW or NNCREW Commercial Real Estate Women or the National Network of Commercial Real Estate Women. Among the major commercial real estate firms are Colliers International, Grubb and Ellis, Staubach, Jones Lang LaSalle, CB Richard Ellis, Marcus and Millichap, Sperry Van Ness, DTZ, and NAI.

Corporate Real Estate

All major corporations must deal with real estate needs. Overall corporate real estate management involves maximizing the value to the firm of the resources devoted to space needs. Once simply viewed as a cost center, corporate real estate managers are now attempting to improve the efficiency of real estate usage by considering "just-in-time" office sharing and enhancing the productivity of the work environment. In addition, corporate real estate heads often deal with site analysis, buy versus lease decisions, acquisition and disposition, portfolio refinancing and sale leaseback arrangements, property tax appeals, and a host of facility management decisions. Many corporations are now outsourcing much of their work to the major brokerage firms such as those listed above.

For more information about corporate real estate see CoreNet Global (formerly IDRC & NACORE).

<u>Development</u>

Among the most entrepreneurial of the real estate career paths are the developers who may acquire land or older property in need of rehabilitation and prepare it for development or in some cases also handle the construction process. Developers specialize in residential or commercial development, and within these they specialize by size and type of property.

Today home builders are getting larger and working more on a regional and national basis. Larger home builders have a number of specialists within a firm or affiliated as subcontracting consultants, such as those that specialize in land acquisition and market analysts, financing developments, project managers and marketing sales staff to name a few. Developers who went through a period of over building in the late 1980's and early 1990's are now actively engaged in burgeoning suburban office and industrial markets. Mixed residential use development is becoming more common and this requires greater expertise than ever.

For more information about residential development see the National Association of Home Builders, NAHB as well as the NMHC the National Multi-Housing Council. For more

information about commercial development opportunities and trends see the Urban Land Institute, ULI, the National Association of Industrial and Office Properties, NAIOP, and the International Council of Shopping Centers, ICSC.
Mortgage and Construction Lending: Mortgage lenders specialize by size of loan and property types much as do developers or commercial brokers. Primary lenders for residential single family include mortgage companies that resell the loans in the secondary mortgage market, as well as commercial banks, savings institutions and credit unions. The banks and savings institutions usually pay employees on a salary basis, sometimes with a bonus. Mortgage companies rely more on productivity based compensation. Loan officers must know about credit analysis as well as appraisal, title and environmental concerns and a host of other government regulations. Multifamily mortgage lenders act much like commercial mortgage lenders with more emphasis on property analysis including market trends, tenant review, income and expense review as well as the value of the subject property being used as collateral. Commercial banks and savings institutions provide most of the smaller multifamily loans while life insurance companies, pension funds, Real Estate Investment Trusts (REIT) and CMBS (collateralized mortgage backed securities) investment bankers and pension funds often provide larger scaled financing.

Non-residential mortgage loans involve commercial banks as well as life insurance companies and pension funds as typical suppliers of capital. Commercial mortgage lenders require more business education and analytical skills than do the residential lenders, often requiring graduate education. Mortgage brokers are often used to represent smaller life insurance companies and pension funds that cannot efficiently process their own loans. Mortgage brokers work on a commission basis paid after successfully placing mortgage loans that meet the needs of the borrower and lender.

Construction lending is the most complicated end of the financing spectrum involving all of the concerns of the permanent mortgage lender (credit, income, expenses, property value and environmental) as well as absorption risk, construction cost risks and delays, and other concerns. Thus, construction lenders are often hired from among the ranks of experienced mortgage lenders. Most construction lending is provided by commercial banks.

In the future we expect more commercial mortgage money to come from securitized capital market instruments like CMBS via capital market investment bankers. For more information about mortgage banking see the Mortgage Bankers Association, or MBAA (profile included in trade associations section.)

Property Management

Property management involves maximizing the net revenues or productivity of property based on managing rental flows, working on tenant retention, managing and contracting for all aspects required to operate a property (cleaning, maintenance and repairs, paying utilities, property insurance, property taxes and so on), reporting to owners and overseeing resident or on site managers. Property managers are usually involved in leasing and facility management decisions. Those that manage several properties and are involved in acquisition, disposition, financing and portfolio management decisions are known as "asset managers." Most property managers start as on-site managers working closely with tenants.

Consolidation is the general trend in the industry; many property management firms are national or international in scope and are able to take over an entire institutional portfolio of various properties from different cities. Property managers' fees are often based on the rental flows of the property, as well as the complexity of the property management work. For example, shopping center property

managers may be involved in tenant merchant associations, joint promotions and advertising which involves much more time than, say, a single tenant industrial property where the primary management function is accounting based control, reporting and monitoring.
For more information about property management see the Building Owners Managers Association, BOMA, and the Institute of Real Estate Management, IREM.

Institutional Real Estate Investment
Most of today's large scale real estate transactions ($10 million dollars and up) involve institutional investors. Among these are the Real Estate Investment Trusts (REITs), larger life insurance companies and pension funds. These institutions may utilize commercial brokers in the local markets but rely on internal staff to review and analyze proposed investments. Often these institutions look for a real estate background and an MBA degree when staffing such positions. Institutional investors pay attention to general industry niche market trends, tax law trends, regulatory trends, local geographically based economic trends, demographic trends and global economic trends in addition to micro level real estate deal analysis.

The slogan "think globally, act locally" can be applied to today's institutional investment firms, and many of them also "act globally." Whether working with domestic or international trusts, strong analytical skills, the ability to manage portfolios and excellent communication skills are required.

For more information see the National Institution of Real Estate Investment Trusts, NAREIT, and the National Association of Real Estate Investment Fiduciaries, NCREIF. Also see RECRA, the Real Estate Capital Resources Association and **PREA**, the Pension Real Estate Association.

There are many other specializations related to the real estate industry; however, the specializations above generally require a business background. Other specializations include design, (see AIA, the American Association of Architects), engineering, law, construction, environmental consulting, real estate tax and regulatory counseling, design review, economic and market feasibility analysis, planning (see the APA, American Planning Association), education and research. Overall, real estate provides many promising career paths.

Choosing a University for the Study of Real Estate

There are many fine real estate programs in the United States as well as in many other industrialized countries. Leading brand name schools including MIT, Wharton, Wisconsin, Berkeley, and Harvard have fine real estate programs, but there are many others that are excellent today and constantly improving. Rather than list out all the other schools (see Part 2 for universities with real estate programs, page 27), consider the following criteria for selecting a program and use the university listings for more research:

- ✓ Faculty noted for their research and publishing
- ✓ Internships and cooperative education jobs encouraged
- ✓ Professional placement assistance and web site support
- ✓ Scholarships for real estate majors
- ✓ Student real estate business organizations provide career exposure
- ✓ Advisory Boards that provide mentoring and career assistance
- ✓ Field trip experiences are available
- ✓ Public schools within the state will generally be lower in tuition costs
- ✓ Courses in related fields are available such as Economic Geography, Geographic Information

Systems (GIS) and Land Use Planning

Looking for Employment in the Real Estate Industry: Advice to Students

Once you have decided on a career path in real estate your job search plan must start well before graduation. Most students seem to think that they should focus only on school, current part time jobs and social life until they near graduation. But, the smart students who will get the greatest number of offers understand that the job search starts as soon as they know which industry appeals to them. Here are some selected tips on how to start the professional search plan:

1. **Join the local university real estate organization** or club, and if one doesn't exist, start one. The National Association of REALTORS has an affiliate known as Rho Epsilon, but there are many independent university groups. For example, at the University of Cincinnati the Real Estate Club is called "Alpha Rho Epsilon" and at Indiana University it is simply the "Real Estate Club" both oriented towards commercial real estate. Become an officer of the organization if possible and become involved in program planning. Not only will becoming an officer look great on your resume, it will give you the opportunity to meet some key real estate professionals. Encourage your real estate group to have as many officer positions as sincere volunteers exists, i.e. President, Vice-President for Programming, Vice-President for Finance, Vice-President for Career Placement, Vice-President for Alumni Relations, and so on. Take advantage of this opportunity to learn about different career paths by inviting speakers from various specialties and arranging field trips to development projects or coordinating a "spend-a-day" or "shadow" program

with local professionals and students. "Mentors" can also be sought from local professionals who are matched up with students one-to-one and encouraged to meet quarterly to review career plans. On the web site that will accompany this book we plan to have a national mentor match up system where volunteer mentors from industry and students can match up.

2. **Join some of the local/regional and national real estate trade associations** and attend their meetings. Most of the trade associations mentioned above allow student participation, often with greatly reduced fees or free. If the local chapters don't have such a policy for discount student affiliation ask them to start one. Keep an address file of all professionals that you meet for potential future use. Consider developing your own business card, even if it purely a personal card, and list your e-mail address on the card as well as your personal web page address that can be accessed for an updated resume.

3. **Try and attend a regional or national conference of one of the above trade associations**. This is most easily accomplished when negotiated on behalf of several students that are part of a university sponsored real estate organization, but most of the professional associations will provide greatly reduced fees for students that want to attend part or all of a major conference. These conferences and dates can be found at the web site for each of the organizations noted above.

4. **Start to "network" with the most promising and impressive of your classmates**. Some day some of your classmates will be potential business partners or colleagues or among those who can influence your business success. Getting to know

these future colleagues now while they are more accessible to you is an opportunity that should not be forsaken. Keep in mind that your performance in the classroom and on cases is something that influences your classmates' future opinions of your abilities as well as your professors.

5. **Try and get to know at least two or more faculty members well** enough that when you are asked for a reference letter you won't panic thinking no one really knows you beyond exam scores or grades. A reference letter that states only grade performance will not do you much good. Professors will get to know you if you join student organizations and participate in activities out of class. They will also get to know you if you speak up in class, ask good questions and prepare well for class. Last, they will get to know you if you take advantage of office hours and review the current class expectations along with some of your personal goals. Most faculty do not mind a little of this personal planning discussion and actually enjoy getting to know their students better.

6. **Once graduation gets closer it makes sense to start sending out letters** along with the resume requesting appointments for career planning advice. If someone has a job they will certainly be responsive to a follow up phone call a few days after receiving a resume. If the recipient has no job prospects, they may still be willing to meeting briefly to review the organization of the industry and leading firms in the area, to which letters might be sent. This is known as an "informational interview" to which industry professionals are much more receptive while a student is still in school. Don't wait for potential employers to call you back. Most won't! It is almost impossible to follow up too much.

7. Prior to a real job interview **spend some time researching the company** and learning about current industry trends. This can be done via the library, local business papers, the internet, and through contacts made while in school. Make sure to develop a set of questions to ask at the appropriate time. Such questions can be as important as the job interview answers in showing real concern for the firm and the position. Self-confidence is critical for all successful interviews. A "can do" attitude is essential. Always follow up interviews with thank you letters and a request for feedback.

8. **Post a resume on Real-Jobs.com** as soon as you are ready for part time jobs or within 12 months of a full time job. Real Jobs is a web site designed to serve the students and alumni of university real estate programs or with a career interests in real estate, as well as potential employers and professionals. Unlike most resume and job posting systems, you can search real-jobs.com by geography, experience, education or other criteria. Post a resume on Real Jobs at the following address: http://www.real-jobs.com.

Further Professional Development

Even after landing a job there is a need to continue to work hard at maintaining skills and knowledge in order to maintain marketability and value to a firm. This requires constantly monitoring what is going on in the local, regional, national, and even global markets within those areas where expertise is claimed.

How does anyone keep up on their field? First, the simple answer is to read, read, and read. Most of this reading will be skimming, with selected in-depth reading. Read local business papers, newsletters from private firms like and trade associations, specialized papers and monographs. Reports from the local City Economic Development office, Chamber of Commerce or other non-profit business organizations might be useful. National periodicals like "National Real Estate Investor", "Commercial Property News", "Shopping Centers Today" from the ICSC, "Development" from NAIOP, "Institutional Real Estate Newsletter", "Area Development: Site and Facility Planning" and many others are good examples of publications that monitor industry trends. Newsletters like those produced by IREI, the Institutional Real Estate Investor, Heitman, Prudential, Fidelity, Legg Mason, Jones Lang LaSalle, the large accounting firms like Deloitte, PricewaterhouseCoopers and many others are also potentially valuable reports. Customized clipping services are also available via the internet where the user subscribes to selected topics of interest and receives selected reports via e-mail and secured subscriber web sites on only the selected topics

Beyond reading "real estate" publications, try and broaden yourself with books and general business or management journals and attend continuing education seminars. These are often required among some states for real estate license maintenance, appraisal certification maintenance or for various real estate designations. These can be a waste of time and money if the sole purpose is license maintenance, but if selected carefully these can be very valuable not only for the direct instruction from speakers but also for the chance to talk to colleagues and share experiences. One or two seminars a year is probably the minimum most professionals need. Consider a professional designation.

Professional Designations

Real estate, more than any other industry, because of its diverse nature, has a cornucopia of professional designations. These include for example:

MAI for Member of the Appraisal Institute
MCR for Master of Corporate Real Estate
CRE for Counselor of Real Estate
CCIM for Certified Commercial Investment Member

Using this Career Resource Guide Effectively
Part 2 (page 27) includes a listing of universities that offer real estate programs and degrees. High school students may use this guide to select an undergraduate program of interest. University students may use this guide for deciding upon graduate education options. Web sites, contact and general program information are provided for all schools listed.

Part 3 (page 97) includes a list of trade associations that offer opportunities for continuing education and professional licensing designations. These resources are often excellent alternatives to a full college degree for those with some business background or experience and an interest in focused or continuing education. Even those professionals with university training in real estate need to maintain this knowledge base and the trade associations listed in this section provide the best place for career updates and advancement.

Part 4 (page 147) presents profiles of commercial real estate professionals, including career background information and advice, compiled by Dr. Margot Weinstein. For more information on these profiles, or extended length interviews please contact Dr. Weinstein (email on page 2) or visit our website (URL forthcoming).

Part 5 (page 229) includes a glossary of real estate terms, including general, office, and industrial related terminology, along with information on how to find more glossaries online.

Part 2

University Real Estate Programs

American University

Website homepage:
http://kogod.american.edu/ArtPage.cfm?ItemID=577

Contact Information:
Kogod School of Business
4400 Massachusetts Avenue NW
Washington, DC USA 20016
Peter Chinloy
chinloy@american.edu
202-885-1951

Private or Public University: Private

About American Real Estate Program:
Washington DC location. Flexible FT and PT MBA degree programs. Undergraduate programs with major & minor in real estate.

Year established: 1966
Degree/Certificate offerings: BBABS, MBA
Length of study: 2 years, MBA
Number of Students: 100
Graduates per year: 20
Faculty & Staff: Full-2

Additional resources found at website:

Faculty
Admissions
Co-op/Internships
Placement
Global Studies
Scholarship/Aid
Tuition
Student Orgs
Advisory Board

California State University - Fullerton

Website homepage: http://cbeweb-1.fullerton.edu/finance/relui/

Contact Information:
800 N. State College Blvd, CP 1060
Department of Finance
Fullerton, CA U.S.A 92834
Donald Valachi
jrer@fullerton.edu
714-278-2217

Private or Public University: Public

About California State University - Fullerton Real Estate Program:
A solid undergraduate degree program in real estate/finance.

Year established: 20
Degree/Certificate offerings: BBABS, Certificate
Length of study: 4 years
Number of Students: 50
Graduates per year: 50
Faculty & Staff: Full-3 Part-time-6

Additional resources found at website:

Faculty
Admissions
Placement
Scholarship/Aid
Tuition
Student Orgs

California State University Northridge

Website homepage: http://busecon.csun.edu/fin

Contact Information:
Dept. of Finance, Real Estate & Insurance
18111 Nordhoff Street
Northridge, CA 91330-8379
Dr. Donald Bleich / Professor
donald.bleich@csun.edu
818-677-2410

Private or Public University: Public

About California State University Northridge Real Estate Program:
The mission of the department is excellence in teaching, research, and service. We serve our students, the academic and business communities, and the public through the production and dissemination of knowledge in the disciplines related to finance, real estate, and insurance. We pursue this in an environment of mutual respect and collegiality.

Degree/Certificate offerings: BSBA
Length of study: 4 or 5 year

Additional resources found at website:

- Faculty
- Requirements
- Co-op/Internships
- Placement
- Scholarship/Aid

Clemson University

Website homepage: http://www.clemson.edu/caah/pla/mred/index.htm

Contact Information:
121 Lee Hall
Clemson, SC 29634-0511
Dr. J. Terrence Farris, CRE, AICP, Program Director
jfarris@clemson.edu
864-656-3903

Private or Public University: Public

About Clemson University Real Estate Program:
The new full-time, 54-credit, two-year professional Master of Real Estate Development (MRED) degree program is jointly offered by the Department of Planning and Landscape Architecture (administrative unit) in the College of Architecture, Arts, and Humanities and the Department of Finance in the College of Business and Behavioral Science with required courses from six disciplines: MBA, Finance, Law, Architecture, Construction Science & Management; and Planning and Landscape Architecture.

The program primarily follows the principles of the Urban Land Institute (ULI), which acknowledges that development is a public-private partnership and that quality development requires integrating the perspectives of community, environment, and economics.

Year established: 2004
Degree/Certificate offerings: Master of Real Estate Development
Length of study: 2 years w/summer internship
Number of Students: 6
Faculty & Staff: Full-4 Part-time-15
Program features: Goal of 20 students annually. This national program is in the heart of the rapidly growing southeast between Atlanta and Charlotte, close to coastal development internship opportunities in Myrtle Beach, Charleston, and Hilton Head.

Additional resources found at website:

Faculty

Admissions

Cleveland State University

Website homepage: http://urban.csuohio.edu

Contact Information:
UR223 Levin College Urban Affairs
Cleveland, OH 44115
Robert A. Simons
roby@urban.csuohio.edu
216-687 5258

Private or Public University: Public

About Cleveland State Real Estate Program:
Our program is a graduate real estate certificate program of urban real estate finance and development. It includes 2 courses in urban planning and 2 courses from the business school. Emphasis is on central city real estate redevelopment finance.

Year established: 1999
Degree/Certificate offerings: Certificate
Length of study: 1-2 years
Number of Students: 15
Graduates per year: 5
Faculty & Staff: Full-2 Part-time-1

Additional resources found at website:

Faculty
Admissions
Student Orgs

Colorado State University

Website homepage: http://www.biz.colostate.edu/ciref

Contact Information:
326 Rockwell Hall
1272 Campus Delivery
Everitt Real Estate Center
Fort Collins, Colorado 80523-1272
Glenn R. Mueller, Ph.D.
glenn.mueller@colostate.edu
970-491-2739

Private or Public University: Public

About Colorado State University Real Estate Program:
Everitt Real Estate Center
Undergraduate concentration in Real Estate & Finance
Major Planned for 2006
Graduate degree planned for 2008

Year established: 1998
Degree/Certificate offerings: BBABS
Length of study: 4 years
Number of Students: 80
Graduates per year: 40
Faculty & Staff: Full-2 Part-time-6
Program features: Industry internships promoted; Strong industry relationships; Fast-growing metro area

Additional resources found at website:

Co-op/Internships

Placement

Scholarship/Aid

Student Orgs

Columbia Business School

Website homepage:
http://www2.gsb.columbia.edu/departments/realestate

Contact Information:
325A 3022 Broadway, Uris Hall
New York, NY 10027
Cheryl Carruthers, Associate Director
cc2263@columbia.edu
212-854-8556

Private or Public University: Private

About Columbia Business School Real Estate Program:
The program comprises three integral elements: a world-class business education with an emphasis on finance, a focused real estate curriculum and strong links with a diverse and accessible concentration of real estate experts. By bringing these professionals together with the students and highly respected, full-time faculty, the program produces analytical thinkers, creative problem solvers and strategic decision makers who are prepared to operate professionally across a spectrum encompassing both local space markets and global asset markets.

Year established: 1978
Degree/Certificate offerings: MBA
Length of study: 2 years
Number of Students: 90
Graduates per year: 35
Faculty & Staff: Full-2 Part-time-5
Program features: The advisory board forms the basis of the Real Estate Forum, a by-invitation association of 39 senior industry professionals, who attend an annual seminar about strategic industry issues, and are involved in teaching, mentoring and case writing. The Center has 70 proprietary cases that are regularly integrated into the curriculum.

Additional resources found at website:

Faculty
Admissions
Placement
Student Orgs
Advisory Board

Cornell University

Website homepage: http://www.realestate.cornell.edu

Contact Information:
Program in Real Estate, 114 West Sibley
Ithaca, New York USA 14853
C. Bradley Olson/Director
jc347@cornell.edu
607-255-7110

Private or Public University: Private

About Cornell University Real Estate Program:
Cornell's Master of Professional Studies in Real Estate (MPS/RE) degree program has the rigor of a traditional MBA program while focusing squarely on the real estate industry. The Program's comprehensive curriculum includes study of principles of real estate, real estate investment and finance, land and project development, asset management, and property marketing and management - combined with exposure to design, engineering, economics, urban planning, and real estate law. The connection between theory and industry practice receives consistent emphasis. Students work together on real-world case studies and other projects to understand and appreciate real estate principles and arrive at reality based solutions

Year established: 1996
Degree/Certificate offerings: MPS (Master of Professional Studies in Real Estate)
Length of study: 2 academic years
Number of Students: 40
Graduates per year: 20
Faculty & Staff: Full-20 Part-time-2
Program features: The course offerings, curriculum, and faculty available to students coupled with a diverse student body, make Cornell's the richest offering of its kind in graduate real estate education. Additional focus on leadership and management issues further prepares students for future industry leadership.

Additional links at www.realestate.cornell.edu:

Faculty	Global Studies	Placement
Admissions	Scholarship/Aid	Advisory Board
Co-op/Internships	Student Orgs	

DePaul University

Website homepage: http://www.realestate.depaul.edu

Contact Information:
Dr. Susanne Canon
DePaul Center, Suite 6070
The Real Estate Center
1 East Jackson
Chicago, IL USA 60604
realestate@depaul.edu
312-362-5906

Private or Public University: Private

About DePaul University Real Estate Program:
The demand for qualified real estate professionals continues to increase as the real estate industry is being transformed by economic, social, regulatory, and demographic factors in Chicago, across the nation, and around the world. At DePaul, we've studied and taught real-estate trends for more than 90 years. In fact, we currently offer the most comprehensive array of real estate courses in Chicago, and the academic and practical qualifications of our faculty allow us to offer an unparalleled real estate education. Courses are frequently team taught by full time faculty and leading Chicago area professionals, with a strong emphasis on case discussion that links theory with pragmatic approaches to problem solving.

Year established: 2002
Degree/Certificate offerings: BBABS, MS, MBA, Certificate
Length of study: 2 year, 4 year

Additional resources found at website:

Faculty
Scholarship/Aid
Student Orgs

EUROPEAN BUSINESS SCHOOL

Website homepage: http://www.ebs-immobilienoekonomie.de

Contact Information:
Schloss Reichartshausen
Oestrich-Winkel, Hesse, Germany 65375
Prof. Dr. Karl-Werner Schulte, HonRICS
immobilienoekonomie@ebs.de
0049 6723 69 151

Private or Public University: Private

About EUROPEAN BUSINESS SCHOOL Real Estate Program:
As a state-recognized private university, European Business School International University (ebs) ranks among the top three universities in Germany for courses on Business Administration. After a foundation in General Business Administration the Department of Real Estate at the European Business Sschool International University offers a specialization in Real Estate. The Department of Real Estate and the ebs IMMOBILIENAKADEMIE form the ebs Real Estate Center which combines three functions: student education, executive education and research & consulting. The Department of Real Estate concentrates on undergraduate education while the focus of the ebs IMMOBILIENAKADEMIE lies on post-graduate and executive education.

Year established: 1990
Degree/Certificate offerings: BBABS, MS, MBA, PhD, Certificate
Length of study: Depending on Degree
Number of Students: 400
Graduates per year: 300
Faculty & Staff: Full-4 Part-time-200
Program features: Full Time, BSc General Management (Real Estate Major), MSc. Real Estate, Part Time, Executive MBA Real Estate, PGC Real Estate Management (RICS accredited), PGC Corporate Real Estate Management & Facilities Management (RICS accredited), PGC Shopping Center Management, PGC Real Estate Portfolio Management, PGC Residential Property Management, PGC International Real Estate Appraisal, Qualification Course to Commercial Member of Appraisal Institute (MAI), English for Real Estate Professionals.

Additional resources found at website:

Faculty Admissions

Florida Atlantic University

Website homepage: http://www.fau.edu/realestate

Contact Information:
College of Business, LA 444
2912 College Avenue
Boca Raton, FL 33314
Real Estate Program Director
561-297-3684

Private or Public University: Public

About Florida Atlantic University Real Estate Program:
Our program is designed to provide the unique knowledge and skills necessary for a successful career in the real estate industry. Our courses focus on developing students' analytical and conceptual abilities for making informed real estate financing, investment, development, management, brokerage (leasing and sales), and valuation decisions.

FAU is fully accredited by the Southern Association of Colleges and Schools (SACS) and the College of Business is fully accredited by the Association to Advance Collegiate Schools of Business (AACSB International).

Degree/Certificate offerings: BBABS, MBA

Additional resources found at website:

Faculty

Admissions

Florida Gulf Coast University

Website homepage: http://cps.fgcu.edu/

Contact Information:
College of Business
10501 FGCU Blvd South
Ft. Myers, FL 33965-6565
H. Shelton Weeks
sweeks@fgcu.edu
239-590-7373

Private or Public University: Public

About Florida Gulf Coast University Real Estate Program:
Executive MBA in Real Estate Development.

Year established: 2005
Degree/Certificate offerings: MBA
Length of study: 24 months
Number of Students: 16
Faculty & Staff: Full-1 Part-time-2

Additional resources found at website:

Faculty
Admissions
Co-op/Internships
Placement
Global Studies
Scholarship/Aid
Tuition
Student Orgs
Advisory Board

Florida State University

Website homepage: http://www.ree.fsu.edu

Contact Information:
Rovetta Business Bldg, Rm 313
Dept. of Risk Mgmt., Real Estate and Business Law
Tallahassee, FL 32306-1110
Dean Gatzlaff, Chair
dgatzla@fsu.edu
850-644-4070

Private or Public University: Public

About Florida State University Real Estate Program:
The real estate program at Florida State University features a comprehensive curriculum that serves as a foundation for students seeking employment in a wide array of real estate-related enterprises. Degreed programs are offered at the graduate (MBA – concentration in real estate) and undergraduate (BS – major in real estate) levels. A graduate certificate program in real estate development is offered to students admitted to the MBA or Urban and Regional Planning programs. The program's primary objective is to provide students with the analytical and decision-making skills to effectively compete in a global real estate market.

Year established: 1974
Degree/Certificate offerings: BBABS, MBA, Certificate,
Length of study: BS - 4 yrs., MBA - 2 yrs., Certificate - 1 yr.
Number of Students: 380
Graduates per year: 165
Faculty & Staff: Full-15 Part-time-2
Program features: The graduate concentration in real estate finance and analysis is offered as part of the online MBA program at FSU. It seeks to enhance the skills and qualifications of working professionals who are unable to attend an on-campus MBA program.

Additional resources found at website:

- Faculty
- Admissions
- Co-op/Internships
- Placement
- Global Studies
- Scholarship/Aid
- Tuition
- Student Orgs
- Advisory Board

Georgia State University

Website homepage: http://www.robinson.gsu.edu/realestate

Contact Information:
1405 35 Broad Street, #1405
Atlanta, GA 30302-4020
Dr. Joseph S. Rabianski, PH.D., CRE - Chairman
realestate@gsu.edu
404-651-2760

Private or Public University: Public

About Georgia State University Real Estate Program:
A broad and highly specialized real estate program with a large full-time faculty, many courses, and small classes. The department curriculum combines the legal and regulatory environment, market analysis techniques, and financial synthesis for a highly practical approach to professional real estate education.

A downtown location provides opportunities for part-time and full-time employment, field trips and guest speakers. Extensive day and evening offerings accommodate employed students and offer rich networking opportunities with fellow students employed in the real estate industry.

Year established: 1956
Degree/Certificate offerings: BBABS, MS, MBA, PhD, Certificate,
Length of study: BBA-4, MBA-1.5, MSRE-1.5, PhD-3-4 years
Number of Students: 317
Graduates per year: 41
Faculty & Staff: Full-6 Part-time-6
Program features: Scholarship money available. Mentoring program. Active Student Real Estate Association. Active Real Estate Alumni Group.

Additional resources found at website:

Faculty	Scholarship/Aid
Admissions	Tuition
Co-op/Internships	Student Orgs
Placement	Advisory Board
Global Studies	

Harvard Graduate School of Design

Website homepage: http://www.gsd.harvard.edu

Contact Information:
Gund Hall
48 Quincy St
Cambridge, MA 01238
Robin Brinckerhoff, Coordinator
rbrincke@gsd.harvard.edu
617-495-2337

Private or Public University: Private

About Harvard Graduate School of Design Real Estate Program:
The Management and Real Estate Studies area covers Project Management, and Real Estate and Urban Development. It addresses professionals who want to pursue further studies on business issues related to the building industry, starting from conceiving the buildings, to the planning and managing of design and construction. Most courses address both US and international projects and are based on case studies, emphasizing a hands-on experience in real world situations requiring judgment and making decisions under conditions of responsibility. Often, the program attracts designers who want to enhance or change their careers but admission is open to students from diverse backgrounds.

Year established: 1986
Degree/Certificate offerings: Master in Design Studies in Real Estate
Length of study: 9 months
Number of Students: 15
Graduates per year: 15
Faculty & Staff: Full-4

Additional resources found at website:

Faculty	Scholarship/Aid
Admissions	Tuition
Co-op/Internships	Student Orgs
Placement	Advisory Board
Global Studies	

Howard University

Website homepage: http://www.howard.edu

Contact Information:
School of Business
Suite 500
2600 6th Street, NW
Washington, District of Columbia 20059
Dr. L. Jide Iwarere
liwarere@howard.edu
202-806-1634

Private or Public University: Private

About Howard University Real Estate Program:
Program is currently downsized to a concentration in the finance major. Graduate program and upgrade of undergraduate offerings are in planning stages.

Year established: 1970
Degree/Certificate offerings: BBABS
Length of study: 4 years
Faculty & Staff: Full-1

Additional resources found at website:

Faculty
Admissions
Co-op/Internships
Placement
Global Studies
Scholarship/Aid
Tuition
Student Orgs
Advisory Board

Indiana University

Website homepage: http://www.indiana.edu/~cres

Contact Information:
746 Kelley School of Business
Bloomington, IN 47405
Jeffrey D. Fisher
fisher@indiana.edu
812-855-7794

Private or Public University: Public

About Indiana University Real Estate Program:
Indiana University Bloomington is a comprehensive research university, attracting top faculty and scholars from around the world and offering personalized learning experiences, including Intensive Freshman Seminars, Freshman Interest Groups, overseas study, the Hutton Honors College, and many other academic programs. Our emphasis on the freshman learning experience was recognized by TIME magazine when it named IU College of the Year among research universities in 2001. The finance/real estate department is in the Kelley School of Business.

Year established: 1932
Degree/Certificate offerings: BBABS, MBA, PhD
Length of study: 2 years for MBA
Number of Students: 30
Graduates per year: 30
Faculty & Staff: Full-1 Part-time-1
Program features: The Indiana University Center for Real Estate Studies provides support of real estate majors in a variety of ways including scholarships, field trips, career assistance and independent study projects.

Additional resources found at website:

- Faculty
- Admissions
- Co-op/Internships
- Placement
- Global Studies
- Scholarship/Aid
- Tuition
- Student Orgs
- Advisory Board

Johns Hopkins University

Website homepage: http://www.spsbe.jhu.edu

Contact Information:
100 N. Charles St. SPSBE, 7th floor
Baltimore, MD 21201
Marie Moineau
mcmoineau@jhu.edu
410-516-0772

Private or Public University: Private

About Johns Hopkins University Real Estate Program:
The Johns Hopkins Master of Science in Real Estate, one of only five multi-disciplinary graduate real estate degrees offered in the country, provides the knowledge and skills needed to analyze, understand, and to take advantage of the latest developments in this fast-changing profession. Whether your specialty is finance, investment analysis, asset management, architecture, banking or law, a Hopkins real estate degree affords you an important, unmatched advantage in today's competitive industry environment.

Two graduate real estate programs: one for mid-career and one for entry level professionals. The mid-career program is offered full or part time in Washington DC or Baltimore. The entry level program is offered in Baltimore and includes a paid internship in a private firm.

Year established: 1989
Degree/Certificate offerings: MS, Certificate
Length of study: 40 credits
Number of Students: 250
Graduates per year: 30
Faculty & Staff: Full-3 Part-time-50

Additional resources found at website:

Faculty	Scholarship/Aid
Admissions	Tuition
Co-op/Internships	Student Orgs
Placement	Advisory Board
Global Studies	

Kellogg School of Management

Website homepage: http://www.kellogg.northwestern.edu/realestate

Contact Information:
6214 Jacobs Hall
Northwestern University
2001 Sheridan Road
Evanston, IL 60208-2001
Teri Murray
tsm@kellogg.northwestern.edu
847-491-3564

Private or Public University: Private

About Kellogg School of Management Real Estate Program:
The real estate program, administered by the Guthrie Center for Real Estate Research, is a comprehensive program designed to ensure that students acquire a basic knowledge of knowledge of finance, development, planning, law and investment – as these topics apply to the real estate profession. The curriculum prepares students for high-level professional and managerial careers in the industry. The Kellogg Real Estate Program addresses all aspects of real estate development – social, economic, and financial. The courses are taught by leading scholars and distinguished practitioners with significant practical experience in the areas real estate and law.

Year established: 1987
Degree/Certificate offerings: MBA
Length of study: Full Time - (2Y, 1Y, MMM, JD-MBA) and Part Time
Number of Students: 3020
Graduates per year: 1030
Faculty & Staff: Full-2 Part-time-4
Program features: In addition to classroom activities, students interact with real estate professionals. This interaction provides both a firm analytical foundation and an applied bridge to professional practice. Kellogg Real Estate Club students participate in an annual real estate conference, competitions between leading business / real estate schools around the country, class project competitions, project site visits, the Real Return Newsletter, professional development and career networking programs, golf outings, and a variety of other social events.

Additional resources found at website:

Faculty Admissions Co-op/Internships Placement

Louisiana State University Shreveport

Website homepage: http://www.lsus.edu

Contact Information:
One University Place, Finance Department
Shreveport, LA 71115
Douglas Bible
dbible@pilot.lsus.edu
318-707-5241

Private or Public University: Public

About Louisiana State University Shreveport Real Estate Program:
Public University located in thriving metropolitan area (population about 400,000) of Northwest Louisiana, three hours from Dallas. Mild climate. Financial Services program includes real estate, AACSB College of Business, class size averages 15-20.

Year established: 20
Degree/Certificate offerings: BBABS
Length of study: 4 years
Number of Students: 50
Graduates per year: 10
Faculty & Staff: Full-27 Part-time-5

Additional resources found at website:

Faculty
Admissions
Scholarship/Aid
Tuition

Marquette University

Website homepage:
http://www.marquette.edu/programs/majors/realestate.shtml

Contact Information:
College of Business Administration, Real Estate Program
Milwaukee, WI 53201
mark.eppli@mu.edu
414-288-5724

Private or Public University: Private

About Marquette University Real Estate Program:
Finding the perfect location is as important to a growing business as hiring the employees to run it. Will a new coffee shop thrive in this neighborhood? What about a condominium or apartment complex? Could this be the right spot for a commercial plant? Businesses may range from tiny storefronts to sprawling industrial complexes, but the importance of commercial real estate — and those who understand it — is the same.

Whether your interest is to work for a firm that invests in, develops or services commercial real estate, or to run your own commercial real estate business, Marquette's new major is a great place to prepare for your career, because you'll learn how to analyze, evaluate, finance, develop and manage commercial real estate.

Year established: 2004
Degree/Certificate offerings: BBABS
Length of study: four years
Number of Students: 25
Faculty & Staff: Full-1 Part-time-2

Additional resources found at website:

Faculty	Scholarship/Aid
Admissions	Tuition

Marylhurst University

Website homepage: http://www.marylhurst.edu

Contact Information:
212 Flavia Hall
17600 Pacific Highway - Hwy 43
P. O. Box 261
Marylhurst, OR 97036-0261
Paul Aragon, Director
paragon@marylhurst.edu
800-634-9982

Private or Public University: Private

About Marylhurst University Real Estate Program:
Located in the suburbs of Portland, Oregon, Marylhurst University is a Catholic based liberal arts university founded in 1893 by the Sisters of the Holy Names of Jesus and Mary. As the oldest Catholic university in Oregon, the university welcomes students of all faiths and backgrounds. Marylhurst is accredited by the Northwest Association of Schools and Colleges and the business programs (including Real Estate) have been initially accredited by the International Assembly of Collegiate Business Education.

Year established: 2001
Degree/Certificate offerings: BBABS, Certificate, BS in Business with a concentration in Real Estate
Length of study: 4 years
Number of Students: 41
Graduates per year: 4
Faculty & Staff: Full-4 Part-time-9
Program features: The entire curriculum of the Real Estate Studies program is available online, accessable 24/7, providing the student with the flexibility to pursue their degree while continuing to pursue their career.

Additional resources found at website:

Faculty	Scholarship/Aid
Admissions	Tuition
Student Orgs	Placement

Massachusetts Institute of Technology

Website homepage: http://web.mit.edu/cre

Contact Information:
77 Massachusetts Ave, W31-310
Cambridge, MA 02139
Jennifer Boyles/ Academic Assistant
jboyles@mit.edu
617-253-8308

Private or Public University: Private

About Massachusetts Institute of Technology Real Estate Program: MIT's MSRED program was the first one-year graduate program in the country to educate men and women in the full range of skills demanded of real estate professionals today. It is recognized worldwide as a leader in the field with almost 600 graduates in responsible positions with leading real estate. The program is distinguished from other graduate-level real estate programs by its 12-month duration and its full access to the university's academic resources. organizations in the United States and abroad.

Year established: 1975
Degree/Certificate offerings: MS
Length of study: 1 year program
Number of Students: 40
Graduates per year: 40
Faculty & Staff: Full-9 Part-time-6
Program features: The curriculum integrates knowledge from each of the major disciplines that contributes to the real estate industry in a rigorous course of study that balances theory with practice and draws heavily upon the relationship with industry which characterizes education at MIT.

Additional resources found at website:

- Faculty
- Admissions
- Placement
- Scholarship/Aid
- Tuition

Mississippi State University

Website homepage: http://www.cbi.msstate.edu

Contact Information:
326 McCool Hall
P. O. Box 9580
Dept of Finance and Economics
Mississippi State, Mississippi 39762
Bill Hardin
bhardin@cobilan.msstate.edu
662-325-7478

Private or Public University: Public

About Mississippi State University Real Estate Program:
MSU offers two real estate related majors in the College of Business and Industry. The first is a major in Real Estate with a focus on real estate decision making and investment. The second major is in Construction Management and Land Development. Approximately 175 students are enrolled in these two majors.

Year established: 1978
Degree/Certificate offerings: BBABS
Length of study: 124 hours (semester)
Number of Students: 175
Graduates per year: 45
Faculty & Staff: Full-2 Part-time-1

Additional resources found at website:

Faculty
Admissions
Co-op/Internships
Placement
Global Studies
Scholarship/Aid
Tuition
Student Orgs
Advisory Board

Morehead State University

Website homepage:
http://www.moreheadstate.edu/business/index.aspx?id=3403

Contact Information:
Combs Bldg. 212 UPO 703
150 University Drive
Morehead, KY 40351
Lary B. Cowart, Ph.D., ASA
l.cowart@morehead-st.edu
606-783-5155

Private or Public University: Public

About Morehead State University Real Estate Program:
The Real Estate Option is designed to prepare students for entrepreneurial and managerial positions in the real estate industry. The program is designed for undergraduate students and real estate practitioners with college level courses to meet the educational requirements for real estate licensing. The program prepares students for careers in appraisal, brokerage, consulting, development, property management, corporate real estate, and related areas.

Year established: 1980
Degree/Certificate offerings: BBABS
Length of study: 27 hours in the major
Number of Students: 65
Graduates per year: 11
Faculty & Staff: Full-1 Part-time-3

Additional resources found at website:

Faculty

Admissions

Scholarship/Aid

New York University

Website homepage: http://www.scps.nyu.edu/rei

Contact Information:
11 West 42nd Street, 509
New York, NY USA 10036
Marcie Burros
marcie.burros@nyu.edu
212-992-3335

Private or Public University: Private

About New York University Real Estate Program:
The NYU Real Estate Institute is one of the world's largest and most dynamic centers for real estate related education. Located in midtown Manhattan, the program provides unparalleled experience with real estate finance, investment and development.

Year established: 1988
Degree/Certificate offerings: MS
Length of study: 4 semesters full-time, 7 semesters part-time
Number of Students: 674
Graduates per year: 180
Faculty & Staff: Full-18 Part-time-60
Program features: Extensive networking opportunities through adjunct faculty, large part-time student population, conferences and student student sponsored events.

Additional resources found at website:

Faculty
Admissions
Co-op/Internships
Placement
Global Studies
Scholarship/Aid
Tuition
Student Orgs

Old Dominion University

Website homepage: http://www.odu.edu/creed

Contact Information:
Constant Hall, CBPA
Norfolk, VA 23529
Jon Crunkleton
DrJonRC@AOL.com
757-683-3584

Private or Public University: Public

About Old Dominion University Real Estate Program:
Undergraduate program designed to prepare students for a wide variety of real estate related professions.

Year established: 1970
Degree/Certificate offerings: BBABS
Length of study: 4 years
Number of Students: 25
Graduates per year: 10
Faculty & Staff: Full-2
Program features: Center for Real Estate and Economic Development

Additional resources found at website:

- Faculty
- Admissions
- Co-op/Internships
- Placement
- Global Studies
- Scholarship/Aid
- Tuition
- Student Orgs
- Advisory Board

Penn State University

Website homepage: http://smeal.psu.edu/

Contact Information:
310 BAB, Penn State
University Park, PA 16801
Austin Jaffe
ajj@psu.edu
814-865-4172

Private or Public University: Public

About Penn State University Real Estate Program:
At undergraduate level, we offer a real estate track in the finance major. Students take 4 finance courses and 2-3 real estate courses. We offer elective courses in the MBA program, and have an active doctoral program

Year established: 1970
Degree/Certificate offerings: BBABS, MBA, PhD
Number of Students: 30
Graduates per year: 30
Faculty & Staff: Full-3 Part-time-2

Additional resources found at website:

Faculty
Admissions
Co-op/Internships
Placement
Global Studies
Scholarship/Aid

Roosevelt University

Website homepage: http://www.roosevelt.edu/realestate

Contact Information:
430 South Michigan Avenue
Chicago, IL 60605
Sofia Dermisi, Asst Professor of Real Estate
sdermisi@roosevelt.edu
312-281-3355

Private or Public University: Private

About Roosevelt University Real Estate Program:
The Chicago School of Real Estate at Roosevelt University is the newest school within the College of Business Administration. The Chicago School of Real Estate's mission is to raise the quality bar within the real estate profession. Our aim is to create career opportunities and enhance the resource base for the industry through a diversified program that attracts the best and the brightest of individuals to the school.

Year established: 2002
Degree/Certificate offerings: MBA, Certificate
Length of study: 2 years
Number of Students: 90
Graduates per year: 30
Faculty & Staff: Full-2 Part-time-1

Additional resources found at website:

Faculty

Admissions

Sauder School of Business at UBC

Website homepage: http://sauder.ubc.ca

Contact Information:
Henry Angus 2053 Main Mall
Vancouver, BC Canada
Tsur Somerville, Professor
tsur.somerville@sauder.ubc.ca
604-822-8343

Private or Public University: Public

About Sauder School of Business at UBC Real Estate Program:
The Sauder School of Business provides for a concentration in real estate as part of the BComm and MBA degrees. Undergraduates take 5 courses in real estate, covering real estate investment, development, finance and urban and real estate economics.

Year established: 1958
Degree/Certificate offerings: BBABS, MBA, PhD, Certificate
Length of study: 4 years

Additional resources found at website:

Faculty

Scholarship/Aid

St. Cloud State University

Website homepage: http://www.stcloudstate.edu

Contact Information:
Herberger College of Business
720 4th Av S
St. Cloud, MN 56320
Good Mooney, PhD
moon@stcloudstate.edu
320-308-4986

Private or Public University: Public

About St. Cloud State University Real Estate Program:
St. Cloud State University is a school of about 15,500 total students. About 25% of those are business majors, and of those about 90 are real estate majors.

Year established: 1980
Degree/Certificate offerings: BBABS, MBA
Length of study: 4 year undergrad degree
Number of Students: 90
Graduates per year: 40
Faculty & Staff: Full-2
Program features: The SCSU Real Estate major is the only real estate major in the state of Minnesota accredited by AACSB.

Additional resources found at website:

Faculty
Admissions
Co-op/Internships
Placement
Global Studies
Scholarship/Aid
Tuition
Student Orgs
Advisory Board

Stephen M. Ross School of Business
University of Michigan

Website homepage: http://www.umich.edu/~reecon/restate/

Contact Information:
701 Tappan Street, D4201
Ann Arbor, MI 48109-1234
Dennis Capozza, Prof. of Finance & Real Estate
capozza@umich.edu
734-764-1269

Private or Public University: Public

About Stephen M. Ross School of Business Real Estate Program:
Dr. Capozza's research activity is currently focused on real estate and consumer finance. Some recent published research includes articles on real investment, capital intensity and interest rates; income taxes and housing prices; why focus matters; the dynamic structure of housing markets; and debt, agency and management contracts in REITs: The external advisor puzzle, inside ownership and q-ratios.

Year established: 1943
Degree/Certificate offerings: BBABS, MBA
Length of study: 4 YRS BBA, 2 YRS MBA

Additional resources found at website:

Faculty
Scholarship/Aid

Temple University

Website homepage: http://www.temple.edu

Contact Information:
SP 206E Department of Finance
Fox School of Business & Management
Philadelphia, PA 19122
Forrest Huffman
fhuffman@temple.edu
215-204-6675

Private or Public University: Public

About Temple University Real Estate Program:
Temple University is a large, urban university located in Philadelphia, PA. The real estate program is located in the Fox School of Business & Management and the Department of Finance. The School offers and undergraduate major in real estate as part of the BBA degree in the Fox School.

Year established: 1970
Degree/Certificate offerings: BBABS
Length of study: 4 year BBA program
Number of Students: 110
Graduates per year: 20
Faculty & Staff: Full-5 Part-time-2
Program features: For information on the student organization for real estate students, the Temple University student chapter of Lambda Alpha International, contact Professor Huffman at fhuffman@temple.edu.

Additional resources found at website:

Faculty
Admissions
Scholarship/Aid
Tuition

Texas Tech University

Website homepage: http://www.ttu.edu

Contact Information:
Rawls College of Business Area of Finance, MS 2101
Lubbock, Texas 79409-2101
Paul Goebel
pgoebel@ba.ttu.edu
806-742-3339

Private or Public University: Public

About Texas Tech University Real Estate Program:
The Rawls College of Business at Texas Tech University offers a BBA degree in Finance with a Specialization in Real Estate. This Specialization provides for a tailoring of the program of study to focus on the functional areas of real estate in a finance context.

Year established: 1980
Degree/Certificate offerings: BBABS
Length of study: 4 years
Number of Students: 60
Graduates per year: 35
Faculty & Staff: Full-1 Part-time-4

Additional resources found at website:

- Faculty
- Admissions
- Co-op/Internships
- Placement
- Scholarship/Aid
- Tuition

The University of Texas at Austin

Website homepage: http://cref.mccombs.utexas.edu

Contact Information:
CBA 6.222 McCombs School of Business
1 University Station B6600
Austin, Texas 78712-1179
Angela Dorsey, Assistant Director
angela.dorsey@mccombs.utexas.edu
512-232-7385

Private or Public University: Public

About The University of Texas at Austin Real Estate Program:
The real estate program of the University of Texas at Austin's McCombs School of Business is supported by the Real Estate Finance & Investment Center as a specialization for currently enrolled business students. Students must first be admitted to the MBA or BBA program at UT. The academic focus of the real estate program is finance & investments as applied to commercial real estate properties, and includes asset valuation, capital market studies, equity & debt financing, and actual commercial case studies with numerous guest speakers from real world practice.

Year established: 1999
Degree/Certificate offerings: BBABS, MBA
Length of study: dependent on MBA or BBA program requirements.
Number of Students: 85
Graduates per year: 45
Faculty & Staff: Full-2 Part-time-3
Program features: National Real Estate Challenge, Real Estate Career Day, Real Estate Career Mentoring Program for students, REIT Competition.

Additional resources found at website:

Faculty	Scholarship/Aid
Admissions	Tuition
Placement	Student Orgs
Global Studies	Advisory Board

Universite du Quebec a Montreal- UQAM

Website homepage: http://www.uqam.ca/

Contact Information:
R-3770 Case postale 8888
Succursale Centre-ville, H3C3P8
Montréal, Québec, Canada
Ünsal Özdilek
ozdilek.unsal@uqam.ca
514-987-3000 x 4436

Private or Public University: Public

About Universite du Quebec a Montreal- UQAM Program:
The UQAM Real Estate Division offers undergraduate and graduate (MBA) programs that serve the needs of the real estate industry at the local, national, and international levels. Our program received the Real Estate Educators Association's Most Outstanding Education Program award in 1990, and shares the international reputation of its Business Administration School.

Year established: 1971
Degree/Certificate offerings: BBABS, MBA, Certificate
Number of Students: 150
Graduates per year: 50
Faculty & Staff: Full-4 Part-time-6
Program features: UQAM's Real Estate education program is recognized provincially and nationally. Successful completion of the Certificate courses (10) grants professional accreditation to practitioners in the industry by the Real Estate Institute of Canada (REIC), and Quebec Assessor's Association, leading also to the recognition of numerous employers, and professional organizations. Our executive MBA program in Real Estate supplies professionals with the expertise and insight required to prosper in today's global markets. Created in 1996, UQAM-SITQ Real Estate Chair offers financial assistance to enrolled students, and organizes annually a Real Estate Forum gathering more than 300 leading actors in the sector.

Additional resources found at website:

Faculty	Placement	Tuition
Admissions	Global Studies	
Co-op/Internships	Scholarship/Aid	

University of Aberdeen

Website homepage: http://www.abdn.ac.uk

Contact Information:
Edward Wright Building Dunbar Street
Aberdeen, Grampian Scotland, UK
Katja Christie
gbs@abdn.ac.uk
+44 (0) 1224 273235

Private or Public University: Public

About University of Aberdeen Real Estate Program:
The MSc Property and MBA Business and Property degrees are intended to be both "fast track" conversion courses for those seeking professional accreditation as well as offering an educational experience based on the cutting edge of international real estate research. The courses are accredited by the Royal Institution of Chartered Surveyors.

Year established: 1970
Degree/Certificate offerings: MBA, PhD, MSc
Length of study: 12 months for MBA/ MSc, 3 years for PhD
Number of Students: 40
Graduates per year: 40
Faculty & Staff: Full-6 Part-time-2
Program features: The Business School also offers a PhD and MPhil program in the Property discipline.

Additional resources found at website:

Admissions

Tuition

University of Alabama

Website homepage: http://www.cba.ua.edu/

Contact Information:
127 Bidgood Hall
P.O. Box 870221
Tuscaloosa, Albama
Leonard Zumpano

Private or Public University: Public

About University of Alabama Real Estate Program:
The University of Alabama offers undergraduate and graduate (MS and MBA) concentrations in real estate. Finance Ph.D. dissertations can also be written on real estate topics.

Year established: 1940
Degree/Certificate offerings: BBABS, MS, MBA
Number of Students: 30
Graduates per year: 8
Faculty & Staff: Full-2 Part-time 3
Program features: The Real Estate Research and Education Center offers employment and job placement assistance for real estate students.

Additional resources found at website:

Faculty

Admissions

University of Cincinnati

Website homepage: www.business.uc.edu/realestate

Contact Information:
Real Estate Program
403 Lindner Hall College of Business
PO Box 210195
Cincinnati, OH 45221-0195
Alison Sampson, Program Manager
real.estate@uc.edu
513-556-7193

Private or Public University: Public

About University of Cincinnati Real Estate Program:
A real estate integral at UC is flexible and broad based, while emphasizing an entrepreneurial spirit. It combines a core curriculum covering the functional areas of business (accounting, economics, finance, information systems, marketing, and operations management) with specialized coursework in real estate. Exposures to other disciplines impacting the field of real estate include construction, geography, planning, and civil engineering. In addition to functional exposure to real estate, the program emphasizes writing, negotiation, oral communication, analytical problem solving, and computer skills.

Year established: 1981
Degree/Certificate offerings: BBA, MBA
Length of study: varies
Number of Students: 180
Graduates per year: 5
Faculty & Staff: Full-3 Part-time-3
Program features: The Real Estate Center also presents the Real Estate Roundtable series, a breakfast lecture series for professionals and students in the real estate industry, and an annual Real Estate Banquet, which draws over 600 professionals from the region.

Additional resources found at website:

- Faculty
- Admissions
- Co-op/Internships
- Placement
- Global Studies
- Scholarship/Aid
- Tuition
- Student Orgs
- Advisory Board

University of Colorado

Website homepage: http://leeds.colorado.edu/realestate

Contact Information:
Leeds School of Business
Room 251 Real Estate Center, 419 UCB
Boulder, CO 80309-0419
Byron Koste/Director
katie.mrazik@colorado.edu
303-492-3643

Private or Public University: Public

About University of Colorado Real Estate Program:
The University of Colorado Real Estate Center is a high-caliber academic real estate program for graduate and undergraduate students attending the Leeds School of Business. The ultimate goal of the program is for the students to graduate with relevant, practical, and meaningful experience that they can apply to a career in real estate. The real estate program offers coursework, internships, networking, mentoring, and job placement assistance. The Center is supported by a group of over 300 real estate industry professionals who desired a stronger relationship between the real estate industry and the University of Colorado.

Year established: 1996
Degree/Certificate offerings: BBABS, MBA, Certificate
Length of study: 2 - 4 years
Number of Students: 550
Graduates per year: 150
Faculty & Staff: Full-4 Part-time-4
Program features: The Center is involved in campus and external University real estate issues; in community land use issues, providing research, advice, and facilitation; and with ULI, NAIOP, CREW, and other industry organizations to provide opportunities for our students and to educate and inform Coloradans about current real estate issues.

Additional resources found at website:

Admissions
Co-op/Internships
Placement
Advisory Board

University of Connecticut

Website homepage: http://www.business.uconn.edu/realestate

Contact Information:
School of Business
Room 402
2100 Hillside Road, Unit 1041RE
Storrs, CT USA 06269-1041
CF Sirmans, Director
recenter@business.uconn.edu
860-486-3227

Private or Public University: Public

About University of Connecticut Real Estate Program:
The Center for Real Estate and Urban Economic Studies was established in 1965 by the Connecticut General Assembly for the purpose of providing professional and practical assessment of real estate issues in Connecticut, the region, and the nation. The UConn Center for Real Estate is ranked #1 in the nation for real estate research and is among the top 10 real estate centers in the U.S. Its impressive academic credentials are matched by a strong emphasis on real-world problem solving. The Center draws from a staff with deep and diverse professional experience. The Center trains highly skilled individuals for all segments of the industry work force; its graduates are nationally renowned leaders guiding major real estate firms.

Year established: 1965
Degree/Certificate offerings: BBABS, MBA, PhD, Certificate
Length of study: 4 yrs undergrad, 2 yrs full time MBA, 5 yrs PhD
Number of Students: 450
Graduates per year: 75
Faculty & Staff: Full-7 Part-time-2

Additional resources found at website:

Faculty	Scholarship/Aid
Admissions	Tuition
Co-op/Internships	Student Orgs
Placement	Advisory Board
Global Studies	

University of Denver

Website homepage: http://daniels.du.edu/burns

Contact Information:
Daniels College of Business
2101 S. University Blvd, #380
Denver, CO 80208
Dr. Mark Lee Levine
mlevine@du.edu
303-871-3432

Private or Public University: Private

About University of Denver Real Estate Program:
The Burns School of Real Estate and Construction Management, firmly entrenched in the Daniels College of Business, is the oldest program of its kind in a college of business. It is a carefully considered pragmatic structure that focuses on real-world, hands-on applications. Our program meets most, or all of the MAI, CCIM, and FIABCI designation requirements. You will get compelling, best-of-class business and industry experience that sets you apart from your peers.

Year established: 1938
Degree/Certificate offerings: BBABS, MS, Certificate, Executive Master's Distance Learning degree
Length of study: 4 years for U-grad/12 months for graduate degrees
Number of Students: 400
Graduates per year: 70
Faculty & Staff: Full-10 Part-time-12
Program features: Distance Learning is available for our Certificate Program or our Executive Master's Degree. Our hands-on practicum program involves our students in all aspects of financing, supervising the construction, marketing and selling a single family home.

Additional resources found at website:

Faculty	Scholarship/Aid
Admissions	Tuition
Co-op/Internships	Student Orgs
Placement	Advisory Board
Global Studies	

University of Florida

Website homepage: http://www.realestate.ufl.edu

Contact Information:
Stuzin Hall 301 - Center for Real Estate Studies
PO Box 117168
Gainesville, FL United States 32611-7168
Pam DeMichele/Director of Admission/Student Svc
DeMichPL@UFL.EDU
352-273-0310

Private or Public University: Public

About University of Florida Real Estate Program:
The Master of Science in Business Administration - Real Estate Program (MRE) is housed in the Warrington College of Business (WCB), Department of Finance, Insurance & Real Estate (FIRE). The degree program and activities are supported by the Center for Real Estate Studies (CRES). This one-year program of study thrives on innovation, a dynamic student body, multidisciplinary curriculum and nationally recognized professors. The MRE programs provides significant opportunity for interaction with and mentoring from high-level working professionals that belong to our highly esteemed Advisory Board, UF Friends and Alumni of Real Estate (UF-FARE) and participation in the Ring Distinguished Speaker Series.

Year established: 1987
Degree/Certificate offerings: MS, Joint Degrees with Law, etc.
Length of study: 1 year
Number of Students: 35
Graduates per year: 30
Faculty & Staff: Full-3 Part-time-7
Program features: The UF CRES Real Estate Advisory Board works continually to advance the quality and visibility of the MRE programs, by participating in student mentoring and placement programs, speaking in the Ring Distinguished Speaker series, and the Capstone Course. Activities initiated and sponsored by the Board include the UF-FARE association and the Spring Board Retreat, and they actively participate in scholarship and endowment fund raising activities.

Additional resources found at website:

Faculty	Tuition	Placement
Admissions	Student Orgs	Advisory Board

University of Georgia

Website homepage: http://www.terry.uga.edu/realestate/

Contact Information:
Terry College of Business, 206 Brooks Hall
Athens, GA 30602-6255
Henry Munneke
realestate@terry.uga.edu
706-542-4290

Private or Public University: Public
About University of Georgia Real Estate Program:
The undergraduate real estate program provides the student with an analytical foundation and a firm understanding of real estate finance, investment, and valuation. The major in real estate is directed toward students planning a career in real estate brokerage, leasing, mortgage lending, investments, management, appraising, or development. The MBA program gives a more general background in all aspects of business with a focus in real estate directed toward advanced concepts and methodology useful for the business professional. The PhD program is designed to prepare students for teaching and research at universities and colleges and for positions in government and business.

Year established: 1952
Degree/Certificate offerings: BBABS, MBA, PhD
Length of study: 4 yrs BBA, 1 or 2 yrs MBA, 3-5 yrs PhD
Number of Students: 185
Graduates per year: 100
Faculty & Staff: Full-4 Part-time-1
Program features: The Terry Real Estate Program has an active Real Estate Society which invites real estate practitioners to discuss current real estate issues and career opportunities with the students. These meetings provide students with an opportunity to interact with real estate practitioners from a variety of areas within the industry. Job placement assistance is provided for undergraduate through the University's career counseling and placement service, while the Terry MBA program offers its own a placement service.

Additional resources found at website:

Faculty	Tuition	Placement
Admissions	Student Orgs	Global Studies
Co-op/Internships	Scholarship/Aid	

University of Guelph

Website homepage: http://www.uoguelph.ca

Contact Information:
Department of Marketing and Consumer Studies, N1G 2W1
Guelph, Ontario, Canada N1G 2W1
Jane Londerville
jlonderv@uoguelph.ca
1-519-824-4120 x53091

Private or Public University: Public

About University of Guelph Real Estate Program:
Established in 1992, Guelph's Bachelor of Commerce, Housing and Real Estate Management program is one of only two such programs in Canada. This program is designed to qualify graduates to meet the high demand for employees in the real estate industry and focuses on developing the analytical, conceptual, and managerial skills required for professional careers in the field of commercial or residential real estate.

Year established: 1992
Degree/Certificate offerings: B.Comm.
Length of study: 4 years
Number of Students: 130
Graduates per year: 25
Faculty & Staff: Full-2 Part-time-2
Program features: Students are exempt from some of the required courses for both the appraisal and real estate licensing accreditations.

Additional resources found at website:

Faculty	Scholarship/Aid
Admissions	Tuition
Co-op/Internships	Student Orgs
Placement	Global Studies

University of Illinois at Chicago

Website homepage: http://www.uic.edu/cba/lgradbiz/

Contact Information:
815 W. Van Buren, Suite 220
Chicago, Illinois 60607-3525
mre@uic.edu
312-996-4573

Private or Public University: Public

About University of Illinois at Chicago Real Estate Program:
The Master of Arts in Real Estate program at the University of Illinois at Chicago combines economics, finance, and urban planning to provide students with a full perspective of the field of real estate. The program takes advantage of UIC's location by emphasizing urban real estate markets and by using metropolitan Chicago as a working laboratory. The program is intended for professionals working in either the private or public sectors that are concerned with real estate and real estate development issues.

Year established: 2004
Degree/Certificate offerings: BBABS, MS, MBA, PhD

Additional resources found at website:

Faculty
Admissions
Co-op/Internships
Placement
Scholarship/Aid
Tuition

University of Missouri-Columbia

Website homepage: http://business.missouri.edu

Contact Information:
Cornell Hall
403 Cornell Hall
Columbia, Missouri USA 65211
Dr. David A. West
westd@missouri.edu
573-882-6373

Private or Public University: Public

About University of Missouri-Columbia Real Estate Program:
MU is the flagship campus of the University of Missouri with over 25,000 students. The MU College of Business has four academic units -- Accountancy, Finance, Management and Marketing -- with 50-60 full time faculty, 3,500 undergraduates, and 300 Masters and PhD candidates. The Finance Department offers majors in Finance & Banking and Real Estate. The primary mission of the College is to excel in teaching and research, all degree programs are fully accredited by the AACSB, and the College occupies a new 150,000 sf state-of-the-art facility. About 30,000 alumni contribute their expertise across the US and worldwide.

Year established: 1965
Degree/Certificate offerings: BBABS
Length of study: Four Years
Number of Students: 80
Graduates per year: 75
Faculty & Staff: Full-2
Program features: The MU Real Estate Program graduates 75 majors annually with emphasis on commercial investing, valuation and appraisal, mortgage banking, leasing, property management and brokerage. Business leaders address classes on various topics. Each year, students accept internships with firms around Missouri, primarily in St. Louis, Kansas City and Columbia.

Additional resources found at website:

Faculty	Scholarship/Aid	Student Orgs
Admissions	Tuition	Advisory Board
Co-op/Internships	Global Studies	Placement

University of Nebraska at Omaha

Website homepage: http://www.unomaha.edu

Contact Information:
RH 515 College of Business Administration
6001 Dodge St.
Omaha, Nebraska USA 68182-0048
Dr. Roger Sindt/Professor
rsindt@mail.unomaha.edu
402-554-2802

Private or Public University: Public

About University of Nebraska at Omaha Real Estate Program:
The College of Business at the University of Nebraska at Omaha provides courses of study leading to the BSBA, MA, MS and MBA degrees. UNO is located in an urban environment and provides both day and evening class offerings. The Real Estate and Land Use Economics Program is located in the College of Business Administration's Economics Department. The program offers academic tracks in both residential and commercial areas. A BSBA degree is offered in these concentrations as well as certificate options.

Year established: 1948
Degree/Certificate offerings: BSBA, Certificate
Length of study: 4 years for BSBA
Number of Students: 55
Graduates per year: 15
Faculty & Staff: Full-2 Part-time-4
Program features: Active real estate club for majors.

Additional resources found at website:

- Faculty
- Admissions
- Co-op/Internships
- Placement
- Global Studies
- Scholarship/Aid
- Tuition
- Student Orgs

University of Nevada Las Vegas

Website homepage: http://liedinstitute.com

Contact Information:
Beam Hall, Room 530
Lied Institute for Real Estate Studies
P.O. Box 456025
Las Vegas, Nevada 89154-6025
Debra March
dmarch@ccmail.nevada.edu
702-895-4492

Private or Public University: Public

About University of Nevada Las Vegas Real Estate Program:
The Lied Institute for Real Estate Studies supports a comprehensive four year Bachelor of Science degree in Business Administration with a real estate major, along with research, scholarships, internships, mentoring program, executive and continuing education, the Certified Graduate Builders Institute, the Commercial Real Estate Certification Program, The Real Estate Roundtables and other extension activities. Through these and other programs, the Institute is responding to the growing needs of the Nevada real estate industry, while building a premier program at the University.

Year established: 1990
Degree/Certificate offerings: BBABS, Certificate
Number of Students: 150
Graduates per year: 20
Faculty & Staff: Full-3 Part-time-3

Additional resources found at website:

Faculty
Admissions
Co-op/Internships
Placement
Scholarship/Aid
Tuition
Student Orgs
Advisory Board

University of North Florida

Website homepage: http://www.unf.edu/ccb/

Contact Information:
Dept. of Accounting and Finance
4567 St. Johns Bluff Rd
Jacksonville, FL 32224
Sidney Rosenberg
srosenbe@unf.edu
904-620-2630

Private or Public University: Public

About University of North Florida Real Estate Program:
UNF offers a BBA in Finance with a concentration in real estate. The Coggin College of Business is an comprehensive urban university, AACSB accredited, which offers a full range of courses at the bachelors and master's level and many opportunities for international educational experiences.

Year established: 1973
Degree/Certificate offerings: BBABS
Length of study: 4 years
Number of Students: 90
Graduates per year: 20
Faculty & Staff: Full-2 Part-time-1

Additional resources found at website:

- Faculty
- Admissions
- Co-op/Internships
- Placement
- Global Studies
- Scholarship/Aid
- Tuition
- Student Orgs

University of Northern Iowa

Website homepage: http://www.uni.edu

Contact Information:
CBB 317 - Real Estate Education Program
Cedar Falls, Iowa 50614-0124
Dr. Arthur Cox
cox@uni.edu
319-273-6986

Private or Public University: Public
About University of Northern Iowa Real Estate Program:
The UNI Real Estate Education Program offers a major and minor in Real Estate. In addition to the required Real Estate coursework there is a strong Finance component to the curriculum which is ideal preparation for a variety of careers in Real Estate. Graduates are successful in careers such as brokerage, mortgage lending, appraisal and analysis, property management and development. The UNI Real Estate Education Program enjoys strong ties with the real estate industry, which further enhances employment opportunities for graduates. Over one-half of real estate students participate in at least one paid internship during their undergraduate career.

Year established: 1989
Degree/Certificate offerings: BBABS
Length of study: 120 semester credit hours
Number of Students: 170
Graduates per year: 40
Faculty & Staff: Full-3 Part-time-3
Program features: There is an active student club with regular meetings at which employers and professional industry associations make presentations about career opportunities. The club makes regular visits to different employers. There are networking opportunities for students and industry professionals at a spring golf outings and fall picnic. There are also career fairs in the fall and spring. The UNI Real Estate Education Program has an extensive scholarship program available to Real Estate majors and Real Estate minors.

Additional resources found at website:

Faculty	Scholarship/Aid	Placement
Admissions	Tuition	Global Studies
Co-op/Internships	Student Orgs	

University of Pennsylvania – Meyerson Design School

Website homepage: http://www.design.upenn.edu/new/real/index.htm

Contact Information:
G23 Meyerson Hall School of Design
Philadelphia, PA 19104-6311
Prof Witold Rybczynski
rybczyns@design.upenn.edu
215-247-3546

Private or Public University: Private

About University of Pennsylvania Real Estate Program:
The Certificate in Real Estate Design & Development is offered to graduate students enrolled in the School of Design master's programs in Architecture, City Planning, Historic Preservation, and Landscape Architecture. The required five courses are taken in the School of Design and in the Wharton School.

Year established: 1997
Degree/Certificate offerings: Certificate
Length of study: 1.5 years
Number of Students: 20
Graduates per year: 10
Faculty & Staff: Full-6 Part-time-1
Program features: Due to excessive demand, the CREDD is only taking applications from students already accepted in a PennDesign master's program.

Additional resources found at website:

Faculty
Admissions
Placement
Scholarship/Aid
Tuition
Student Orgs

University of Pennsylvania at Wharton

Website homepage: http://realestate.wharton.upenn.edu

Contact Information:
Steinberg-Dietrich Hall Ste. 1400
3620 Locust Walk
Philadelphia, PA 19104-6302
Janice Leberman/Executive Assistant to the Director
lebermaj@wharton.upenn.edu
215-898-3824

Private or Public University: Private

About University of Pennsylvania Real Estate Program:
The real estate department and the Zell/Lurie Real Estate Center at The Wharton School of the University of Pennsylvania are home to a distinguished faculty. Real Estate at Wharton is a recognized leader in teaching and research involving real estate finance and economics, urban and housing economics, design, real estate law, and public policy affecting real estate issues. The Center's resources, consisting of permanent endowments and annual support from over two hundred member corporations, support faculty and students engaged in a variety of research venues.

Year established: 1983
Degree/Certificate offerings: BBABS, MBA, PhD
Length of study: Four year undergrad, two year MBA
Number of Students: 157
Graduates per year: 77
Faculty & Staff: Full-17 Part-time-8
Program features: The Zell/Lurie Real Estate Center mounts two major programs per year that attract hundreds of real estate industry executives from across the US and other parts of the world. Best in Nation according to U.S. News & World Report, Business Week, Financial Times. Fellowships available; also through Zell-Lurie Real Estate Center. Real Estate Clubs. On-line resume book.

Additional resources found at website:

Faculty	Scholarship/Aid	Global Studies
Admissions	Tuition	Advisory Board
Placement	Student Orgs	

University of San Diego

Website homepage: http://www.usdrealestate.com

Contact Information:
Olin Hall 108, 5998 Alcala Park
San Diego, CA 92110
Lisa Chambers
lchambers@sandiego.edu
619-260-4150

Private or Public University: Private

About University of San Diego Real Estate Program:
In just 50 years, the University of San Diego has grown from a local college with 50 students and a handful of professors to a nationally ranked university. This achievement is the direct result of a single, unwavering expectation of academic excellence within a values-based education. Students choose from more than 60 undergraduate and graduate degree programs including the Master of Science in Real Estate and the International Master of Business degree. Located in beautiful, tropical San Diego, USD adds depth to its education by inspiring students to grow spiritually, morally, socially.

Year established: 1993
Degree/Certificate offerings: BBABS, MS, MBA
Length of study: 11 months
Number of Students: 24
Graduates per year: 30
Faculty & Staff: Full-9 Part-time-9
Program features: The MSRE degree offers a curriculum that develops the specialized skills needed by real estate professionals through an interactive approach. The program provides students with the leadership, communication, and interpersonal skills necessary to compete for real estate careers at the middle- to upper-management levels or to become real estate entrepreneurs.

Additional resources found at website:

Faculty
Admissions
Co-op/Internships
Placement
Global Studies
Scholarship/Aid
Tuition
Student Orgs
Advisory Board

University of South Carolina

Website homepage: http://mooreschool.sc.edu/moore/sccre/

Contact Information:
Moore School of Business
Columbia, SC 29205
Ronald Rogers
rrogers@moore.sc.edu
803-777-5960

Private or Public University: Public

About University of South Carolina Real Estate Program:
The South Carolina Real Estate Center's primary purpose is to enhance professionalism in the real estate industry through applied research and dissemination of information on real estate issues. An Advisory Committee, composed of leaders in the real estate industry, advises the Center. An important function of the Committee is to identify significant and timely issues, determine priorities, and allocate resources. Through a grant program, the Center sponsors research projects on those issues and disseminates the results through a variety of means as a service to the real estate industry. Future plans include specialized executive education courses and conferences on topics of special interest to the real estate industry.

Year established: 1969
Degree/Certificate offerings: BBABS, MBA, PhD

Additional resources found at website:

Faculty

Admissions

Advisory Board

University of Southern California

Website homepage: http://www.usc.edu/lusk

Contact Information:
650 Childs Way, Ste. 331
Los Angeles, CA USA 90089-0626
Sonia Savoulian
sonias@usc.edu

Private or Public University: Private

About University of Southern California Real Estate Program:
USC offers both undergraduate and masters-level real estate degrees:
BS Business Administration with a Real Estate Concentration (4 year degree)
MBA with a Real Estate Concentration (2 year degree)
Master of Real Estate Development (11 month degree)

Degree/Certificate offerings: BBABS, MBA, MRED
Length of study: 1, 2, 4 years
Faculty & Staff: Full-6 Part-time-28
Program features: The USC Lusk Center for Real Estate is a university-wide research center which supports the academic mission of USC real estate degree programs conferred by the Marshall School of Business and the School of Policy, Planning, and Development.

Additional resources found at website:

Faculty
Admissions
Student Orgs
Advisory Board

University of St. Thomas

Website homepage:
http://www.stthomas.edu/realestate/degrees/default.htm

Contact Information:
Shenehon Center for Real Estate Education
1000 LaSalle Avenue, TMH 153
Minneapolis, MN USA 55403
Dr. Tom Hamilton
twhamilton@stthomas.edu
651-962-5551

Private or Public University: Private

About University of St. Thomas Real Estate Program:
The University of St. Thomas (UST) is a comprehensive, coeducational, Catholic university. Founded in 1885, St. Thomas is now the largest private university in Minnesota. Dedicated to providing a career-oriented, values-centered education in a stimulating environment, UST serves more than 10,000 graduate and undergraduate students in our academic programs each year.

Year established: 1995
Degree/Certificate offerings: BBABS, MS, Mini MBA in Real Estate
Number of Students: 125
Graduates per year: 30
Faculty & Staff: Full-2 Part-time-5
Program features: The real estate program at St. Thomas is the only four-year program of its kind offered in the Twin Cities, and you will be prepared to practice real estate and provide ethical, professional leadership.

Additional resources found at website:

Faculty
Admissions
Co-op/Internships
Student Orgs

University of Texas at San Antonio

Website homepage: http://business.utsa.edu/

Contact Information:
Department of Finance
6900 North Loop, 1604 West
San Antonio, Texas USA 78249-0637
Dr. Ronald Rutherford
CONMGT@utsa.edu
210-458-5957

Private or Public University: Public

About University of Texas at San Antonio Real Estate Program:
The Construction Management program provides an alternative to a degree in either business or architecture by combining classes from both disciplines. A graduate from this program will have a wider perspective of the business and architectural aspects of developing a project and will be aware of all phases of the construction process.

While at UTSA, the student's classes will be in general business preparation; i.e., accounting, economics, business law, finance, marketing and real estate. In addition to those courses, there will also be architectural instruction in construction management, cost estimation, design analysis, construction materials, and site analysis.

Degree/Certificate offerings: BBABS, BBA in Construction Management
Length of study: 4 years
Number of Students: 75
Graduates per year: 12
Faculty & Staff: Full-2 Part-time-3

Additional resources found at website:

Faculty	Global Studies
Admissions	Scholarship/Aid
Co-op/Internships	Tuition
Placement	Student Orgs

University of the Pacific

Website homepage: http://www.pacific.edu

Contact Information:
Eberhardt School of Business
3601 Pacific Avenue
Stockton, California USA 95219
John R. Knight/Professor
jknight@pacific.edu
209-946-2637

Private or Public University: Private

About University of the Pacific Real Estate Program:
Real Estate students at Pacific earn a Bachelor of Science in Business Administration with a concentration in Real Estate. Courses include real estate finance, real estate valuation and investments, and real estate law. Pacific is located 80 miles east of San Francisco, and is the oldest chartered private university in the state of California.

Year established: 1995
Degree/Certificate offerings: BBABS
Length of study: 4 years
Number of Students: 30
Graduates per year: 15
Faculty & Staff: Full-2

Additional resources found at website:

Faculty

Admissions

University of Washington

Website homepage: http://reuw.washington.edu

Contact Information:
3949 15th Avenue NE
PO Box 355740
Seattle, WA USA 98195
James R. DeLisle/Director
jdelisle@u.washington.edu
206-616-2090

Private or Public University: Public

About University of Washington Real Estate Program:
The Department of Urban Design and Planning already offers a master's level Concentration in Real Estate to graduate students in planning (MUPs) and other programs from across campus who satisfy certain course requirements. This program is designed to provide students with a real estate specialization within their graduate degree programs.

Year established: 2002
Degree/Certificate offerings: Certificate, MSRE in 2006/2007
Length of study: 24 credits
Number of Students: 40
Graduates per year: 20
Faculty & Staff: Full-2 Part-time-1
Program features: The proposed Master of Science in Real Estate (MSRE) extends the current curriculum by adding more strategic components and providing more depth to help prepare students to take leadership positions in the real estate industry and closely related fields.

Additional resources found at website:

Faculty
Admissions
Co-op/Internships
Placement
Tuition
Student Orgs

University of West Georgia

Website homepage: http://www.westga.edu/~mktreal

Contact Information:
1601 Maple St.
College of Business, 170
Carrollton, GA USA 30118
James H. Burton
jburton@westga.edu
678-839-5023

Private or Public University: Public

About University of West Georgia Real Estate Program:
Our Real Estate program prepares students for careers in all aspects of Commercial and Residential Real Estate, including Sales and Marketing; Appraising; Brokerage; Mortgage Banking; and Investment Analysis.

Qualified juniors and seniors have a chance to work on internships with local businesses, enroll in our summer study-abroad program and to join the local student chapter of the American Marketing Association (The Marketing Club). Our department is strongly committed to the university's philosophy of educational excellence in a personal environment, and our highly qualified faculty makes every effort to ensure the success of our students.

Degree/Certificate offerings: BBABS, MBA
Length of study: 4 yr
Number of Students: 100
Graduates per year: 20
Faculty & Staff: Full-2

Additional resources found at website:

Faculty
Admissions
Co-op/Internships
Global Studies
Scholarship/Aid
Tuition
Student Orgs

University of Wisconsin

Website homepage: http://www.bus.wisc.edu/realestate

Contact Information:
5262 Grainger Hall
Department of Real Estate and Urban Land Economics
975 University Avenue
Madison, WI USA 53706-1323
Stephen Malpezzi, Department Chair
smalpezzi@bus.wisc.edu
608-262-9816

Private or Public University: Public

About University of Wisconsin Real Estate Program:
UW's Real Estate Program dates back to the 1920s, and has a rich history under the leadership of notables such as Richard Ely, Richard Ratcliff, and James Graaskamp. UW's full service program includes Bachelor's, Master's, and the Ph.D. in Real Estate. UW offers a broad curriculum with some 20 courses in all aspects of real estate development and finance. A strong alumni network and active student Real Estate Club provide extracurricular support, including regular field trips.

Degree/Certificate offerings: BBABS, MBA, PhD, Certificate
Length of study: Varies by program. 2 year MBA.
Number of Students: 210
Graduates per year: 115
Faculty & Staff: Full-9 Part-time-9
Program features: In addition to core courses in urban economics, finance and investments, and development, the program features international real estate, including field trips, and the Applied Real Estate Securities Program in which students manage an actual portfolio.

Additional resources found at website:

Faculty	Scholarship/Aid
Admissions	Tuition
Co-op/Internships	Student Orgs
Placement	Advisory Board
Global Studies	

University of Wyoming

Website homepage: http://www.uwyo.edu

Contact Information:
1000 E. University Avenue
Department 3275
Laramie, WY USA 82071
John Downham
real-est@uwyo.edu
307-766-2363

Private or Public University: Public

About University of Wyoming Real Estate Program:
The Real Estate Certificate Program does not require previous training in real estate and is designed for both the student and professional. The certificate program can be part of a degree program or a stand-alone course of study. While sections of these classes are available on campus, they are also offered over the Internet. Courses will be offered so the program can be completed in a year. The program consists of six, three-credit hour classes: three classes in real estate, one in real estate law, and two in the finance and economics fields. Enrollment at the University of Wyoming is not required.

Year established: 2000
Degree/Certificate offerings: Certificate
Length of study: 1 year
Number of Students: 120
Graduates per year: 30
Faculty & Staff: Full-1 Part-time-2

Additional resources found at website:

Faculty

Virginia Commonwealth University

Website homepage: http://realestate.bus.vcu.edu

Contact Information:
Business Building - 5174
1015 Floyd Avenue
PO Box 844000
Richmond, Virginia USA 23284-4000
David H. Downs
dhdowns@vcu.edu
804-828-1721

Private or Public University: Public

About Virginia Commonwealth University Real Estate Program:
The real estate program at VCU provides the student with a comprehensive education foundation with a thorough understanding in related disciplines including development, finance, investments, law, and valuation so that graduates' analytical skills and ability to communicate with other professionals are enhanced. By majoring in real estate students are well prepared for a career in real estate appraising, brokerage, development, investments, mortgage lending, or property and portfolio management. The MS in real estate valuation is approved by the Appraisal Institute which leads to the MAI designation.

Year established: 1973
Degree/Certificate offerings: BBABS, MBA, Certificate
Length of study: 1 to 4 years
Number of Students: 70
Graduates per year: 30
Faculty & Staff: Full-5 Part-time-7

Additional resources found at website:

Faculty	Scholarship/Aid
Admissions	Tuition
Co-op/Internships	Student Orgs
Placement	Advisory Board
Global Studies	

Virginia Tech

Website homepage: http://www.iddl.vt.edu

Contact Information:
3046 Torgersen Hall
Institute for Distance & Distributed Learning, 445
Blacksburg, VA United States 24061
Angie Starr
vto@vt.edu
540-231-1264

Private or Public University: Public

About Virginia Tech Real Estate Program:
Residential Real Estate Development
Delivered in two (2) online courses to cover Single Family and Multifamily, taught by Virginia Tech Associate Professor, Flynn Auchey. These courses use a case study approach for taking undeveloped real estate properties from planning stage, to site engineering, to marketing a finished residential development. Topics covered include: market influences, working with regulatory agencies, zoning, economic considerations, developing an optimum plan, cost risk and schedule, engineering requirements, environmental impact, financing, and delivering a final product.

Year established: 2005
Degree/Certificate offerings: CEU credits
Length of study: Cost: $495 for either module (4 CEU) or $745 for both
Faculty & Staff: Full-1
Program features: Single and Multi Family modules complete and ready to offer for CEU credit. Commercial Development module under development for future offering.

Additional resources found at website:

Faculty	Scholarship/Aid
Admissions	Tuition
Co-op/Internships	Student Orgs
Placement	Advisory Board
Global Studies	

Wichita State University

Website homepage: http://realestate.wichita.edu

Contact Information:
311A Clinton Hall Center for Real Estate
1845 Fairmount
Wichita, KS USA 67260-0077
Stanley D. Longhofer, Director
realestate@wichita.edu
316-978-7120

Private or Public University: Public

About Wichita State University Real Estate Program:
Wichita State offers the only four-year real estate degree in the state of Kansas. Furthermore, our program is unique in that students can obtain this degree through four different major departments--Economics, Entrepreneurship, Finance, or Marketing--allowing students to tailor their coursework to suit their particular career goals. The program provides extensive contact with area real estate professionals, giving students a head start on their professional careers.

Year established: 1978
Degree/Certificate offerings: BBABS
Length of study: 4 years
Number of Students: 60
Graduates per year: 10
Faculty & Staff: Full-2 Part-time-2

Additional resources found at website:

- Faculty
- Admissions
- Co-op/Internships
- Placement
- Global Studies
- Scholarship/Aid
- Advisory Board

York University

Website homepage: http://www.schulich.yorku.ca

Contact Information:
Schulich School of Business, 4700 Keele Street
Toronto, Ontario, Canada
James McKellar
jmckellar@schulich.yorku.ca
416-736-5967

Private or Public University: Public

About York University Real Estate Program:
The Real Property Program is one of several specialized programs available to MBA students who may enrol in either a concentration (four courses) or the Diploma Program (six courses plus an internship/ research requirement) in addition to the MBA. The Program offers six graduate courses in real estate and one undergraduate course. Courses cover finance and investment, portfolio theory, development, market analysis, the legal framework and comparative international markets. The Program has an active student association and alumni group.

Year established: 1992
Degree/Certificate offerings: MBA, Diploma in Real Property
Length of study: 2 years
Number of Students: 35
Graduates per year: 20
Faculty & Staff: Full-2 Part-time-4
Program features: The Wall Street Journal Ranks Schulich Among World's Top International Business Schools. 2004 Financial Times Ranks Schulich School of Business Among World's Top 25 MBA Programs. The Economist Intelligence Unit ranked Schulich 22nd in the world. Ranked among the top six schools in the world in the field of corporate social responsibility by the World Resources Institute and the Aspen Institute. Forbes ranked Schulich 6th in the world outside the US in its international ranking.

Additional resources found at website:

Faculty	Placement	Tuition
Admissions	Global Studies	Student Orgs
Co-op/Internships	Scholarship/Aid	Advisory Board

Part 3

Trade Associations and Professional Organizations

SPONSOR

AI

Appraisal Institute

Website homepage: www.appraisalinstitute.org

Contact Information:
550 W. Van Buren St, Suite 1000
Chicago, IL 60607
312-335-4100
wwoodburn@appraisalinstitute.org

Appraisal Institute®
Professionals Providing Real Estate Solutions

Membership: 18,000
Local Chapters? yes - more than 99 chapters

About AI:
The Appraisal Institute is an international membership association of professional real estate appraisers throughout the United States, Canada and abroad. Its mission is to support and advance its members as the choice for real estate solutions and uphold professional credentials, standards of professional practice and ethics consistent with the public good. The Appraisal Institute is a leader in residential and commercial real estate appraisal education, research. publishing and professional membership designation programs. Its extensive curriculum of courses and seminars provides a well-rounded education in valuation methodology for both the novice and seasoned practitioner. The Appraisal Institute is the publisher of 'The Appraisal Journal' and 'Valuation Insights & Perspectives.' AI grants the designations Member of the Appraisal Institute (MAI), and Senior Residential Appraiser (SRA).

Disciplines served: Appraisal

Membership fees: $310 Associate; $190 Affiliate; $50 Student; company-wide rates are also available

Membership requirements: *Associate membership* is open to appraisers who are performing work governed by the Uniform Standards of Professional Appraisal Practice (USPAP), and may be pursuing the Appraisal Institute's prestigious MAI and SRA designations. *Affiliate membership* is open to individuals who are interested in the Appraisal Institute and the appraisal profession, in related disciplines such as developers, attorneys, and lenders.

SPONSOR **Additional resources found at www.appraisal institute.org:**

Education

Meetings

Research – Lum Library

Publications

Government affairs

Job Bank

Scholarships

AI Minorities & Women Educational Scholarship Program

Eligibility: Applicant must be female or a member of a racial or ethnic minority. Applicant must be a full or part time-student pursuing a degree in real estate or a related field within a degree-granting college/university or junior college/university. Applicants must have proof of a cumulative GPA of no less than 2.5 on a 4.0 scale. Applicant must have demonstrated financial need.

Amount: Up to $2,500

Application: Applications require: an official student transcript; a 500-word essay stating why applicant should be awarded the scholarship based on their academic and professional goals; an attestation that the scholarship will be applied toward tuition/books expenses; two letters of recommendation from previous employers and/or college professors.

Deadline: April 15, 2006 for 2006/2007 academic year.

More information: Applications and current scholarship program information are available from Alison Gerlach, Appraisal Institute, 550 W. Van Buren St., Suite 1000, Chicago IL 60607 or at www.appraisalinstitute.org.

AIA

American Institute of Architects

Website homepage: www.aia.org

Contact Information:
1735 New York Ave., NW
Washington, DC 20006-5292
infocentral@aia.org

Membership: over 75,000
Local Chapters? Yes

About AIA:
Since 1857, the AIA has represented the professional interests of America's architects. As AIA members, over 74,000 licensed architects, emerging professionals, and allied partners express their commitment to excellence in design and livability in our nation's buildings and communities. The American Institute of Architects is the voice of the architecture profession dedicated to: Serving its members, Advancing their value, and Improving the quality of the built environment. Through a culture of innovation, The American Institute of Architects empowers its members and inspires creation of a better built environment.

Disciplines served: Architecture, Design, Engineering

Membership fees: $147.00

Membership requirements: License or degree in architecture; Additional membership categories for those in related professions.

Additional resources found at www.aia.org:

- Education
- Meetings
- Research
- Publications
- Government affairs
- Job Bank
- Scholarships

AIC

Appraisal Institute of Canada

Website homepage: www.aicanada.ca

Contact Information:
203-150 Isabella Street
Ottawa, Ontario K1S 1V7
613-234-6533

Membership: 4500
Local Chapters? Yes

About AIC:
The Appraisal Institute of Canada grants professional designations in real estate appraisal. The Appraisal Institute of Canada is a self-regulating body and, maintains the highest standards, practices and professional conduct in real estate appraisal to protect the public interest.

Disciplines served: Appraisers

Membership fees:

Membership requirements:

Additional resources found at www.aicanada.ca :

Meetings
Research
Job Bank

ALTA

American Land Title Association

Website homepage: www.alta.org

Contact Information:
1828 L Street, NW Suite 705
Washington, DC 20036
800-787-ALTA
service@alta.org

Membership: 2,000 active members
Local Chapters? No

About ALTA:
The American Land Title Association, founded in 1907, is the national trade association and voice of the abstract and title insurance industry. ALTA members search, review and insure land titles to protect home buyers and mortgage lenders who invest in real estate. ALTA is headquartered in Washington, DC. Nearly all title insurance companies hold ALTA membership, in addition to abstracters and title agents. Active members range from small, one-county operations, to large national title insurers. Associate members of ALTA may include attorneys, builders, developers, lenders, real estate brokers, surveyors, consultants, educational institutions, computer services firms, and related national trade associations.

Disciplines served: Title agents, abstracters, underwriters

Membership fees: start at $400, based on gross revenues

Membership requirements: Professionals in title industry and those that provide services to title industry

Additional resources found at www.alta.org:

Education
Meetings
Research
Publications
Government affairs

APA

American Planning Association

Website homepage: www.planning.org

Contact Information:
1776 Massachusetts Ave., NW
Washington, DC 20036-1904
202-872-0611
CustomerService@planning.org

Membership: 37,000
Local Chapters? yes

About APA:
APA is a nonprofit public interest and research organization committed to urban, suburban, regional, and rural planning. APA and its professional institute, the American Institute of Certified Planners, advance the art and science of planning to meet the needs of people and society. The need for planners to shape a community vision has never been greater. The American Planning Association brings together thousands of people — practicing planners, citizens, elected officials — committed to making great communities happen.

Disciplines served: Planning professionals

Membership fees: start at $191

Membership requirements: Planning professional or student

Additional resources found at www.planning.org:

Education
Meetings
Research
Publications
Government affairs
Job Bank
Scholarships

ARES

American Real Estate Society

Website homepage: www.aresnet.org

Contact Information:
Florida Atlantic University College of Business
5353 Parkside Drive
Jupiter, FL 33458
561-779-8594
dcooper@fau.edu

Membership: 900
Local Chapters? no

About ARES:
Founded in 1985, the American Real Estate Society (ARES) is an association of real estate thought leaders. Members draw from academia and the profession at large, both in the U.S. and internationally. ARES is dedicated to produce and disseminate knowledge that is related to real estate decision making and the functioning of real estate markets. ARES' five journals, 'Journal of Real Estate Research,' 'Journal of Real Estate Literature,' 'Journal of Real Estate Portfolio Management,' 'Journal of Real Estate Practice and Education' and 'Journal of Housing Research' provide relevant and timely research of interest to real estate academics and professionals everywhere. ARES is open to anyone with an interest in real estate research. This includes academics in a wide variety of fields such as economics, finance, marketing, geography, and other areas, as well as professional researchers, analysts, appraisers, and others.

Disciplines served: Academics, researchers

Membership fees: Professional $225, Academic $110, Student $55

Membership requirements: Open to anyone with an interest in real estate research

Additional resources found at www.aresnet.org :

Meetings

Research

Publications

Job Bank

AREUEA

The American Real Estate & Urban Economics Association

Website homepage: www.areuea.org

Contact Information:
PO Box 9958
Richmond, VA 23228
866-273-8321
areuea@areuea.org

Membership: 750
Local Chapters? no

About AREUEA:
The American Real Estate and Urban Economics Association (AREUEA) originated at the 1964 meeting of the Allied Social Science Association in Chicago. The continuing efforts of this non-profit association has advanced the scope of knowledge in these disciplines and has facilitated the exchange of information and opinions among academic, professional and governmental people who are concerned with urban economics and real estate issues. AREUEA's journal, 'Real Estate Economics,' is published quarterly and contains research and scholarly studies of current and emerging real estate issues. AREUEA holds three conferences each year on the most up-to-date research available in the fields of real estate and urban economics.

Disciplines served: All real estate related disciplines

Membership fees: $100 (Student $50)

Membership requirements: Open to all individuals and institutions

Additional resources found at www.areuea.org :

Education
Meetings
Research
Publications

ASHI

American Society of Home Inspectors

Website homepage: www.ashi.org

Contact Information:
932 Lee Street, Suite 101
Des Plaines, Illinois 60016
1-800-743-ASHI (2744)
webmaster@ashi.org

Membership: 6000
Local Chapters? yes

About ASHI:
The American Society of Home Inspectors (ASHI) was established with the goal of building consumer awareness and enhancing the professionalism of the field. Home buyers, sellers, real estate professionals and home inspectors alike recognize our resources, educational programs, our Standards and Ethics and our newest program, the ASHI Experience as models of professionalism and superior customer service. We welcome you and invite you to join us in shaping the future of the home inspection profession.

Disciplines served: Home Inspectors

Membership fees: $375

Membership requirements: Must apply as a candidate with record of inspections; then approved for full membership

Additional resources found at www.ashi.org :

Education
Meetings
Publications
Job Bank

AUREO

Association of University Real Estate Officials

Website homepage: www.aureo.org

Contact Information:
North Carolina State University
Box 7230 Raleigh, NC 27695-7230
512-499-4336
klibersat@utsystem.edu

Membership: Over 200 institutions
Local Chapters? No

About AUREO:
AUREO was established in October 1983 as a small, informal, unincorporated organization of about 25 institutions. Its member institutions now represent most major universities in the United States and Canada. AUREO's purpose is to advance by lawful means the common interests of colleges and universities relating to real estate administration, including management, leasing, investment, development, acquisition and disposition.

Disciplines served: Academic and educational professionals

Membership fees: $100

Membership requirements: Real estate official or staff at an educational institution

Additional resources found at www.aureo.org :

Education
Meetings
Research

BOMA

Building Owners & Managers Association International

Website homepage: www.boma.org

Contact Information:
1201 New York Ave. N.W. Suite 300
Washington, D.C. 20005
202-408-2662
info@boma.org

Membership: 19,000
Local Chapters? yes

About BOMA:
BOMA International was founded in 1907 as the National Association of Building Owners and Managers. The association assumed its present name in 1968 as it broadened its reach to include Canada and other affiliates around the globe. The mission of the Building Owners and Managers Association International is to enhance the human, intellectual and physical assets of the commercial real estate industry through advocacy, education, research, standards and information. BOMA International is the premier real estate advocacy group and serves as the government watchdog for national real estate industry issues. It publishes BOMA.org magazine, sponsors an annual conference, and provides educational programs for its members.

Disciplines served: Building owners, investors, property managers, and related professions.

Membership fees: Varies by local chapter.

Membership requirements: Real Estate professionals and companies or individuals that provide goods or services to the real estate industry.

Additional resources found at www.boma.org :

Education
Meetings
Research
Publications
Government affairs
Job Bank
Scholarships

SPONSOR

CCIM Institute

Website homepage: www.ccim.com

Contact Information:
430 N Michigan Avenue, Suite 800
Chicago, IL 60611-4092
312-321-4460
info@ccim.com

Membership: 17,000
Local Chapters? yes

About CCIM:
The CCIM Institute grants the Certified Commercial Investment Member (CCIM) designation and is an affiliate of the National Association of Realtors (NAR). Local chapters and regions represent and actively promote the CCIM designation and curriculum throughout North America, Asia and Europe. The CCIM network is a powerful vehicle for developing business throughout the world, maintaining relationships with other prominent real estate organizations nationally and internationally.

The CCIM curriculum represents the core knowledge expected of commercial investment practitioners, and consists of four core courses that incorporate the essential CCIM skill sets: financial analysis, market analysis, user decision analysis, and investment analysis for commercial investment real estate. A Certified Commercial Investment Member (CCIM) is a recognized expert in the disciplines of commercial and investment real estate.

Disciplines served: The CCIM membership network mirrors the increasingly changing nature of the industry and includes brokers, leasing professionals, investment counselors, asset managers, appraisers, corporate real estate executives, property managers, developers, institutional investors, commercial lenders, attorneys, bankers and other allied professionals.

Membership fees: $495 annual dues

Membership requirements: Must apply for candidacy and take a course towards the CCIM designation

Additional resources found at www.ccim.com :

Education
Meetings
Research
Publications
Government affairs
Job Bank
Scholarships

Benefits of Candidacy

- CCIM Course Discounts – Significant savings on the core designation courses.
- Access to the Site To Do Business – a powerful online business resource site for commercial investment practitioners
- Subscription to CCIMNet – the premier commercial information exchange system for property listings
- Subscription to *Commercial Investment Real Estate (CIRE)* magazine– bimonthly industry-leading publication
- Elective credits towards the CCIM Designation – one elective credit for each consecutive year of candidacy
- Exclusive access to student records to review grades and update contact information

CCIM Designation Requirements at a Glance

Students must complete the following requirements to earn the CCIM designation:

- Become a Candidate of the Institute
- Successfully complete all four core courses (CI 101, CI 102, CI 103, CI 104)
- Earn three elective credits - Elective credits can be earned through a variety of sources, such as completing the CCIM Intro course or attending the Core Concepts Review course.
- Prepare and submit the Portfolio of Qualifying Experience
- Pass the Comprehensive Exam

CoreNet Global

CoreNet Global

Website homepage: www.corenetglobal.com

Contact Information:
260 Peachtree St., Ste. 1500
Atlanta, GA 30303
404-589-3200 Toll Free: 800-726-8111
sdumas@corenetglobal.org

Membership: 7000
Local Chapters? yes

About CoreNet Global:
CoreNet Global is a world-wide association for corporate real estate and related professionals. Programs and services are designed to meet the business needs of members' companies and the career needs of individual members. CoreNet Global was created from the integration of the former International Development Research Council (IDRC) and The International Association of Corporate Real Estate Executives (NACORE International) in 2002 to become the single voice for the industry. CoreNet Global designs its learning programs to rapidly capture, package and deploy new information and business models. CoreNet Global grants the designations Masters in Corporate Real Estate (MCR) and Senior Leader in Corporate Real Estate (SLCR).

Disciplines served: Corporate real estate professionals

Membership fees: $595 End user (Corporate professional) ; $750 Service Provider (related discipline); $95 Academic, student or media

Membership requirements: Corporate real estate professional, related discipline or educator.

Additional resources found at www.corenetglobal.com :

- Education
- Meetings
- Research
- Publications
- Job Bank

CoStar Group

SPONSOR

CoStar: Commercial Real Estate Information Leader

Website homepage: www.costar.com

Contact Information:
2 Bethesda Metro Center, 10th Floor
Bethesda, MD 20814-5388
800-204-5960 or 301-215-8300
info@costar.com

About CoStar Group:
CoStar Group, Inc. is the leading for-profit provider of information services to commercial real estate professionals in the United States and the United Kingdom. CoStar operates the commercial real estate industry's largest researched database of commercial real estate, including detailed property information, for lease listings, for sale listings, sale comparables and tenant information. CoStar services cover the following commercial property categories: office, industrial/flex and retail space for lease; office, industrial/flex, retail, multifamily, hospitality and commercial land for sale. CoStar's customers include commercial real estate broers, property owners, investors, lenders, asset managers, appraisers and vendors allied to the commercial real estate industry.

COSTAR GROUP SERVICES ARE PERFECT FOR:
- Brokers
- Asset managers
- Mortgage lenders
- Investors
- Owners
- Property managers
- Security analysts
- REIT professionals
- Appraisers
- Mortgage Underwriters
- CRE Service Providers

CoStar services can quickly & easily:
- Find the ideal space for tenants
- Match your criteria to find properties for sale
- Find the right tenants from a database of over 3 million in-depth profiles
- Convince prospects you know your markets
- Show prospects how you can save them money
- Analyze market conditions and set winning property positions
- Produce professional presentations and custom reports

SPONSOR

- Stay on top of your markets with late-breaking news
- Reach top brokers in the digital marketplace with free property listings
- Gain thousands more exposures every month with premium banner ads
- Identify confirmed sales information on properties sold in major US markets
- Accurately value commercial real estate sales transactions to reduce risk

CRE

The Counselors of Real Estate

Website homepage: www.cre.org

Contact Information:
430 North Michigan Avenue
Chicago, IL 60611-4089
312-329-8427
info@cre.org

Membership: 1100
Local Chapters? yes

About CRE:
The Counselors of Real Estate is a professional membership organization established exclusively for leaders in real estate property counseling. Real estate counseling is the act of providing advice or guidance on real estate decision-making for a client or employer. The advice is rendered solely for the use of the parties receiving the advice, and it is rendered without personal bias or conflict of interest. The purpose of the organization is to advance, enhance, and support these leaders by serving as a resource for information, by creating opportunities for professional development, and by facilitating networking. All members must adhere to a strict Code of Ethics and Standards of Professional Practice. Members are granted the Counselor of Real Estate (CRE) designation in recognition of their achievements in real estate counseling, after meeting requirements for education and experience in the field.

Disciplines served: Primarily real estate advisors

Membership fees: $1250

Membership requirements: CRE is an invitation-only organization

Additional resources found at www.cre.org :

- Education
- Meetings
- Research
- Publications

CREW

Commercial Real Estate Women

Website homepage: www.crewnetwork.org

Contact Information:
1201 Wakarusa Dr. Ste, C3
Lawrence, KS 66049
785-832-1808
lindah@crewnetwork.org

Membership: 4500
Local Chapters? yes

About CREW:
CREW Network is focused on advancing the success of women in commercial real estate by looking outward to bring more women into the industry, showcasing member successes and serving as a resource to its members and the industry. CREW leads the way with programs like CREW Careers: 'Building Opportunities,' developed to introduce young women to Commercial Real Estate. CREW Network works actively toward creating an environment to facilitate the exchange of information, develop business contacts and help its members succeed professionally and personally.

Disciplines served: All real estate disciplines

Membership fees: Varies by chapter

Membership requirements: Individuals typically join at the local chapter level. Active members must be engaged in the real estate profession with at least two years experience.

Additional resources found at www.crewnetwork.org :

- Education
- Meetings
- Government affairs
- Job Bank
- Scholarships

EAA
Environmental Assessment Association
Website homepage: http://iami.org/eaa.htm

Contact Information:
1224 North Nokomis NE
Alexandria, Minnesota 56308
320-763-4320
eaa@iami.org

Membership: 5000
Local Chapters? yes

About EAA:
The Environmental Assessment Association (EAA) is an international organization dedicated to providing members with information and education in the real estate industry in respect to environmental inspections, testing and hazardous material removal. EAA represents over 5,000 environmental professionals consisting of environmental inspectors, lenders and hazardous material testing and remediation firms and government agencies.

The Environmental Assessment Association offers five designations, and memberships for attorneys and lenders; making the Association the largest in the world for environmental professionals.

Disciplines served: Environmental professionals, suppliers of environmental products and related disciplines

Membership fees: $195

Membership requirements: Must be in field

Additional resources found at http://iami.org/eaa.htm **:**

- Education
- Meetings
- Publications
- Job Bank

FIABCI

International Real Estate Federation

Website homepage: www.fiabci.com or www.fiabci-usa.com

Contact Information(USA):
2000 N. 15th Street
Arlington, VA, USA 22201
703-524-4279
info@fiabci-usa.com

Membership: Over one million
Local Chapters? Yes

About FIABCI:
FIABCI, the International Real Estate Federation, is local, national, and worldwide. Established over 50 years ago, the International Real Estate Federation (FIABCI) is the only truly international organization of its kind in the world. Comprised of professionals in all areas of the industry, FIABCI's long-standing and highly respected presence in the international community gives members instant accessibility, credibility, and dependability. Through individual and association members in 57 countries, FIABCI membership gives access to 1.5 million potential contacts. FIABCI-USA is the only international real estate organization representing the entire spectrum of the real estate industry in the US.

Disciplines served: All aspects of the industry

Membership fees: $555

Membership requirements: Must be either a member of AI, BOMA, CCIM, CORFAC, CRS, HBI, IREM, NAR, SIOR, or sponsored by a member.

Additional resources found at www.fiabci-usa.com :

- Education
- Meetings
- Publications
- Scholarships

HIF

Housing Inspection Foundation

Website homepage: http://www.iami.org/hif.html

Contact Information:
1224 North Nokomis NE
Alexandria, Minnesota 56308
320-763-6350
hif@iami.org

Membership: n/a
Local Chapters? No

About HIF:
The Housing Inspection Foundation (HIF) is an organization of professionals dedicated to the promotion and development of Home Inspection. The Housing Inspection Foundation was created to provide members with Information, Education, Standards, Ethics, and Professional Recognition.

One of the primary objectives of the Housing Inspection Foundation is to provide a network through which its members may establish reliable contacts throughout the country. Designations are available through HIF as a Registered Home Inspector (RHI), Certified Housing Consultant (CHC) and Certified Home Inspector (CHI).

Disciplines served: Home Inspectors

Membership fees: $195

Membership requirements: Must have experience or education in field of Home Inspection.

Additional resources found at: http://www.iami.org/hif.html
Publications
Job Bank

HMBA

Hotel and Motel Brokers of America

Website homepage: www.amhbnetwork.com

Contact Information:
5151 North 16th St.
Phoenix, Arizona 82016
602-230-9244
info@amhbnetwork.com

Membership: Not a membership organization.
Local Chapters? no

About HMBA: American Motel Hotel Brokers Network (commonly known as AMHB Network) is a website for professional real estate brokers/agents that are experienced specialists in the brokering of hotels, motels, resorts, casinos, bed 'n breakfast, and assisted living care facilities for sale throughout the United States, and in Foreign Countries.

American Motel Hotel Brokers (AMHB) is the oldest and best recognized brand name used in the marketing of lodging and hospitality properties for sale.

This web site presents to those that use it, information that people cannot find on any other site. By using today's most modern technology this type of simple yet very much needed material is available. Century 22 will be adding additional services and products.

Additional resources found at: www.amhbnetwork.com

Education
Meetings
Job Bank
Publications

Homer Hoyt Institute

SPONSOR

The Hoyt Group

Website homepage: www.hoyt.org

Contact Information:
760 U.S. Highway One, Suite 300
North Palm Beach, FL 33408
561-694-7621
info@hoyt.org

Membership: Not a membership organization
Local Chapters? No

About Homer Hoyt Institute:
The Homer Hoyt Institute is an independent, non-profit research and educational foundation established in 1968 which contributes to improving the quality of public and private real estate decisions. Hoyt Advisory Services and the Hoyt Institute of Real Estate (HIRE) are wholly-owned subsidiaries of the Homer Hoyt Institute which are utilized for research and development, asset management, and other special assignments. Homer Hoyt Advanced Studies Institute (ASI) operates the Weimer School of Advanced Studies in Real Estate and Land Economics, which recognizes, encourages, and further educates leading real estate decision-makers in academia and industry.

Disciplines served: Academia, Industry and the Public Sector

Membership fees: n/a

Membership requirements: Not a membership organization. Fellows by invitation only.

Additional resources found at www.hoyt.org :

Education
Research
Publications
Scholarships

IAAO

International Association of Assessment Officers

Website homepage: www.iaao.org

Contact Information:
314 West 10th St.
Kansas City, MO 64105-1616
816-701-8100
daniels@iaao.org

Membership: n/a
Local Chapters? yes

About IAAO:
IAAO will be the internationally recognized leader and preeminent source for innovation, education, and research in property appraisal, assessment administration, and property tax policy. We will serve the profession by developing the standards, techniques, and procedures used to maintain accurate property values; the research programs to remain preeminent; the education programs to teach others; the programs for professional designation of assessment personnel to recognize excellence; and the technical assistance and research programs to be the international source for property appraisal, assessment administration, and property tax policy.

Disciplines served: Ad valorem or property assessment professionals and others with an interest in property taxation

Membership fees: starting at $175

Membership requirements: Various categories of membership available.

Additional resources found at: www.iaao.org

- Education
- Meetings
- Research
- Publications
- Scholarships

ICSC

International Council of Shopping Centers

Website homepage: www.icsc.org

Contact Information:
1221 Avenue of the Americas
New York, NY 10020-1099
646-728-3800
icsc@icsc.org

Membership: 50,000
Local Chapters? yes

About ICSC:
Founded in 1975, the International Council of Shopping Centers (ICSC) is the global trade association of the shopping center industry. The principle aims of ICSC are to advance the development of the shopping center industry and to establish the individual shopping center as a major institution in the community. ICSC works on establishing codes of fair business ethics and encourages research on the design and management of shopping centers. This association funds studies of economic, marketing and promotional conditions affecting the shopping center industry. Members of ICSC are considered reputable specialists in the field of shopping center development and management.

Resources: Marketing Analysis/Consulting

Membership fees: $800 private; $100 public

Membership requirements: must be engaged within discipline

Additional resources found at www.icsc.org :

- Education
- Meetings
- Research
- Publications
- Government affairs
- Job Bank
- Scholarships

IREM

Institute of Real Estate Management

Website homepage: www.irem.org

Contact Information:
430 North Michigan Avenue
Chicago, IL 60611
800-837-0706
custserv@irem.org

Membership: 17,500
Local Chapters? yes

About IREM:
The Institute of Real Estate Management (IREM) has been the source for education, resources, information and membership for real estate management professionals for more than 70 years. IREM is an international organization that serves serves both the multi-family and commercial real estate sectors as an advocate on issues affecting the real estate management industry. IREM promotes ethical real estate management practices through its credential membership programs, including the Certified Property Manager (CPM) designation, the Accredited Residential Manager (ARM) certification, and the accredited Management Organization (AMO) accreditation. These esteemed designations certify competence and professionalism for those engaged in real estate management. IREM publishes *The Journal of Property Management.*

Disciplines served: Real Estate Management Professionals

Membership fees: $195 Associate Membership

Membership requirements: Associate membership is open to anyone in the real estate management profession; CPM, ARM and AMO memberships require levels of certification.

Additional resources found at www.irem.org :

- Education
- Meetings
- Publications
- Government affairs
- Scholarships

IRWA

International Right of Way Association

Website homepage: www.irwaonline.org

Contact Information:
19750 South Vermont Ave., Suite 220
Torrance, CA 90502-1144
310-538-0233
info@rwaonline.org

Membership: 8300
Local Chapters? yes

About IRWA:
A "right of way" is a strip of land on which highways, railroads, pipeline, power lines, wireless transmission towers, urban renewal, parks, forestry, wildlife reserves, public buildings, and so forth can be built. Thee amount of land devoted to right of way and public use, for whatever purpose, can be viewed as a direct reflection of the dynamic nature and constantly changing demands of society. Since its inception as a not-for-profit association in 1934, the International Right of Way Association has united the efforts of its members toward individual development, improved service to employers and the public, and advancement in the body of knowledge related to the professional tasks of its members. The IRWA is the only professional association that is the pre-eminent source of right of way educational and professional services worldwide.

Disciplines served: Engineers, Appraisers, Property Managers, Lawyers, Surveyors, Title Experts, and Environmentalists

Membership fees: start at $195

Membership requirements: Must be engaged in profession

Additional resources found at www.irwaonline.org :

Education
Meetings
Research
Publications
Job Bank

LAI

Lambda Alpha International

Website homepage: www.lai.org

Contact Information:
214 North Hale Street
Wheaton, IL 60187 USA
630-510-4584
tgoodnson@association-mgmt.com

Membership: n/a
Local Chapters? yes

About LAI:
Lambda Alpha International, the Honorary Society for the Advancement of Land Economics, was founded in 1930 under the leadership of the renowned land economist and champion of academic freedom, Richard T. Ely. As an honorary society, it provides a forum for the study and advancement of land economics where the "winnowing and sifting" of ideas takes place in an atmosphere of mutual respect.

The Society is now a catalyst for the advancement of land economics by facilitating the interaction of members who have distinguished themselves in their professions, their communities and through academic achievements. Lambda Alpha International provides an opportunity for distinguished practitioners and scholars to come together in fellowship to discuss, debate and perhaps solve dilemmas involving use of our land resources.

Disciplines served: Economics, architecture, civil engineering, geography, landscape architecture, urban planning, public administration, law, environmental design, historic preservation

Membership fees: varies by chapter; $125 for at-large membership

Membership requirements: Must be sponsored by active member and have minimum 10 years experience

Additional resources found at www.lai.org**:**

Meetings

Research

Scholarships

MBAA

Mortgage Bankers Association of America

Website homepage: www.mbaa.org

Contact Information:
1919 Pennsylvania Ave., NW
Washington, DC 20006-3404
202-557-2700
communications@mbaa.org

Membership: 2,700 member companies
Local Chapters: no

About MBAA:
The Mortgage Bankers Association is the national association representing the real estate finance industry. The association works to ensure the continued strength of the nation's residential and commercial real estate markets; to expand homeownership prospects through increased affordability; and to extend access to affordable housing to all Americans.

The MBA seeks to create an environment that enables its members to invest in communities and achieve their business objectives; by developing innovative business tools, educating and training industry professionals, providing a gathering place for the sharing of ideas, acting as the industry's voice on legislative and regulatory issues, and developing open and fair standards and practices for the industry.

Disciplines served: Commercial, residential, and multifamily

Membership fees: Dues based on business volume

Membership requirements: Membership is by company only

Additional resources found at www.mbaa.org :

Education
Meetings
Research
Publications
Government affairs
Job Bank

NAHB

National Association of Home Builders

Website homepage: http://nahb.org

Contact Information:
1201 15th Street, NW
Washington, DC 20005
800-368-5242, 202-266-8200
http://www.nahb.org/contact_us_form.aspx?sectionID=178

Membership: 220,000
Local Chapters? yes

About NAHB:
NAHB is a large Washington, D.C.-based trade association whose mission is to enhance the climate for housing and the building industry. Chief among NAHB's goals is providing and expanding opportunities for all consumers to have safe, decent and affordable housing. About one-third of NAHB's members are home builders and/or remodelers. The remaining members are associates working in closely related fields within the housing industry, such as mortgage finance and building products and services. NAHB analyzes policy issues, takes the industry's story to the public, monitors and works toward improving the housing finance system, and analyzes and forecasts economic trends. The association also represents the industry's interests on Capitol Hill and strives to ensure that housing remains a national priority when laws are made and policies are established.

Disciplines served: Housing industry

Membership fees: Check local home builders association

Membership requirements: Must be engaged in home building industry.

Additional resources found at www.nahb.org :

Education
Meetings
Publications
Job Bank

NAHRO
National Association of Housing and Redevelopment Officials
Website homepage: www.nahro.org

Contact Information:
630 Eye Street, NW
Washington DC 20001
877-866-2476
nahro@nahro.org

Membership: 20,000
Local Chapters? Yes

About NAHRO:
The National Association of Housing and Redevelopment Officials (NAHRO) is the leading housing and community development advocate for the provision of adequate and affordable housing and strong, viable communities for all Americans—particularly those with low- and moderate-incomes. Our members administer HUD programs such as Public Housing, Section 8, CDBG and HOME.

Disciplines served: Housing agencies, Community agencies, developers, and related building trades

Membership fees: Membership is primarily agency-based

Membership requirements: Must work for public housing agency or be engaged in related discipline

Additional resources found at www.nahro.org :

- Education
- Meetings
- Research
- Publications
- Government affairs
- Job Bank

SPONSOR

NAIOP

National Association of Industrial and Office Properties

Website homepage: www.naiop.org

Contact Information:
2201 Cooperative Way 3rd Floor
Herndon, VA 20171
703-904-7100
membership@naiop.org

Membership: 13,000
Local Chapters? yes - 50 throughout North America

About NAIOP:
NAIOP is a national association with more than 13,000+ members and an extensive network of 50 chapters that represent the interests of developers and owners of industrial, office and mixed-use commercial real estate throughout North America. NAIOP provides communication, networking and business opportunities for all real estate related professionals; provides a forum for continuing education; and promotes effective public policy, through its grassroots network, to create, protect and enhance property values.

Disciplines served: Office, industrial and mixed-use real estate

Resources: Numerous networking, education, government affairs and informational resources at both the national and chapter levels

Membership fees: Varies by chapter location. Special fees for students and young professionals.

Membership requirements: Interest and involvement in commercial real estate

Additional resources found at: www.naiop.org

Education
Meetings
Research
Publications
Government affairs
Job Bank
Scholarships

NAMA

National Association of Master Appraisers

Website homepage: http://www.masterappraisers.org/

Contact Information:
303 W Cypress Street
San Antonio, Texas 78212
800-229-6262
djd@lincoln-grad.org

Membership: n/a
Local Chapters? yes

About NAMA:
The National Association of Master Appraisers was organized in 1982 and quickly grew to become one of the major real estate appraisal associations in the United States. NAMA members come from many backgrounds and fields of expertise. Among the ranks of NAMA members are residential, commercial, farm, and land appraisers. Other NAMA members specialize in special types of properties, from manufactured housing to complex commercial and industrial properties. Some also perform specialized services for their clients such as appraising machinery and equipment, doing relocation appraisals and real estate counseling. Others are review appraisers or perform environmental services. NAMA is truly an association of a broad spectrum of the appraisal profession.

Disciplines served: Real estate appraisal professionals

Membership fees: $60; $120; $180

Membership requirements: Interest in profession and completion of coursework in USPAP

Additional resources found at http://www.masterappraisers.org/ **:**

- Education
- Meetings
- Scholarships

NAR

National Association of Realtors

Website homepage: http://www.realtor.org

Contact Information:
430 North Michigan Avenue
Chicago, IL 60611-4087
805-557-2300
infocentral@realtor.org

Membership: Over one million
Local Chapters? yes

About NAR:
Since its inception in 1908, the National Association of REALTORS® has worked successfully to advance home ownership, real estate investment, private property rights and the free enterprise system in the halls of Congress and the Federal agencies. The core purpose of the National Association of REALTORS® is to help its members become more profitable and successful. Today, the National Association of REALTORS® is widely recognized as one of America's strongest, most effective lobbying organizations. NAR's Research Division analyzes the economic, policy and structural effects of changes in the real estate and the ownership and management of real estate firms. NAR publishes 'REALTOR Magazine' and sponsors www.REALTOR.com , a commercial website for real estate listings.

Disciplines served: REALTORS®, both residential and commercial

Membership fees: Varies by local board of realtors

Membership requirements: Contact your local board of realtors

Additional resources found at www.realtor.org **:**

- Education
- Meetings
- Research
- Publications
- Government affairs

NAREA

National Association of Real Estate Appraisers

Website homepage: http://www.iami.org/narea.htm

Contact Information:
1244 North Nokomis NE
Alexandria, Minnesota 56308
320-763-7626
marea@iami.org

Membership: 3500
Local Chapters? no

About NAREA:
The National Association of Real Estate Appraisers (NAREA) is a Professional Organization founded in 1966, making available highly qualified Real Estate Appraisers to those requiring Professional Appraisal Reports. NAREA has earned the credibility and public trust one needs when affiliating with a professional organization. The Code of Ethics and Uniform Standards of Professional Appraisal Practice gives the industry the assurance it needs when accepting an appraisal report from a NAREA designated member. NAREA grants the credentials Certified Real Estate Appraiser (CREA) and Certified Commercial Real Estate Appraiser (CCREA) to qualified members. Along with educational seminars and an annual Appraisal Expo and Conference, members receive bimonthly newsletters, appraisal guidelines, and updates on regulations affecting the Appraisal industry.

Disciplines served: Appraisal

Membership fees: $215

Membership requirements: Must be state licensed or certified real estate appraiser or property consultant

Additional resources found at http://www.iami.org/narea.htm **:**

Education
Publications
Job Bank

NAREB

National Association of Real Estate Brokers

Website homepage: www.nareb.com

Contact Information:
9831 Greenbelt Road
Lanham, Maryland 20706

Membership: n/a
Local Chapters? yes

About NAREB:
NAREB is a national trade association dedicated to bringing together the nation's minority professionals in the real estate industry to promote the meaningful exchange of ideas about our business and how best to serve our clientele. NAREB is the oldest minority trade association in America, founded in 1947.

We strive to create an environment where creativity flourishes in both the workplace and the marketplace. We teach, live by, and search for the highest professional and ethical principles. In this way we can offer economic improvement for both our members and the minority community we serve. When you become a member of NAREB, you will remain abreast of all the latest developments affecting real estate through our publications, meetings, and workshops.

Disciplines served: Minority real estate professionals

Membership fees: n/a

Membership requirements: Open to all real estate professionals

Additional resources found at www.nareb.com **:**

- Education
- Meetings
- Research
- Publications
- Government affairs
- Job Bank
- Scholarships

NAREIA

National Real Estate Investors Association

Website homepage: www.nationalreia.com

Contact Information:
525 West 5th Street, Suite 230
Covington, KY 41011
1-888-762-7342
membership@NationalREIA.com

Membership: 20,000
Local Chapters? yes

About NAREIA:
The National Real Estate Investors Association is a 501(c)6 trade association. Made up of local associations or investment clubs throughout the United States, NAREIA represents local investor associations, property owner associations, apartment associations, and landlord associations on a national scale. NAREIA is the largest broad based organization dedicated to the individual investor.

Founded in 1993, National REIA was born out of a need for more education, networking, and recognition for those individuals who were struggling to grow their local Real Estate Investment group. We are intent on serving the interests of our affiliated groups while maintaining high levels of professionalism within our industry.

Disciplines served: Local investor and property owner associations

Membership fees: Check with your local REIA group

Membership requirements: Check with your local REIA group

Additional resources found at www.nationalreia.com **:**

- Meetings
- Publications

NAREIT

National Association of Real Estate Investment Trusts
Website homepage: www.nareit.com

Contact Information:
1875 Eye Street, NW Suite 600
Washington, DC 20006
202-739-9400
info@NAREIT.com

Membership: 2,000 REITs
Local Chapters? no

About NAREIT:
NAREIT is the national trade association for U.S. REITs and publicly traded real estate companies. Members are real estate investment trusts (REITs) and other businesses that own, operate and finance income-producing real estate, as well as those firms and individuals who advise, study and service these businesses.

NAREIT provides numerous programs, publications and services to its members as well as to nonmembers. Although nonmembers are eligible for several important educational and networking resources, members are entitled to additional benefits and cost savings noted on the website.

Disciplines served: REITs

Membership fees: vary by category

Membership requirements: must be engaged within discipline

Additional resources found at www.nareit.com **:**

- Education
- Meetings
- Research
- Publications
- Government affairs
- Job Bank

NARPM

National Association of Residential Property Managers

Website homepage: www.narpm.org

Contact Information:
P.O. Box 140647
Austin, TX 78714-0647
800-782-3452
Info@NARPM.org

Membership: 2000
Local Chapters? no

About NARPM:
NARPM is the only national organization focused primarily on Residential Property Management. NARPM is an association of real estate professionals who know first-hand the unique problems and challenges of managing single-family and small residential properties. NARPM offers an effective, professional learning environment for owners of property management companies, property managers, and their support staff, whose mission is to support the professional and ethical practices of rental home management through networking, education and certification.

Disciplines served: Residential rental property managers

Membership fees: $195

Membership requirements: Must be engaged in discipline

Additional resources found at www.narpm.org**:**

Education

Meetings

Publications

NCREIF

National Council of Real Estate Investment Fiduciaries

Website homepage: www.ncreif.com

Contact Information:
180 North Stetson Ave. Suite 2515
Chicago, IL 60601
312-819-5890
bleagle@ncreif.org

Membership: 200 companies represented; 35 academic

Local Chapters? No

About NCREIF:
NCREIF was established to serve the institutional real estate investment community as a non-partisan collector, processor, validator and disseminator of real estate performance information.

NCREIF serves this community by assuring that NCREIF data meet the highest quality standards attainable and is published in a timely and efficient manner, serving as a major connecting link between the real estate industry and the real estate research community. Also by bringing the real estate asset class information and disclosure practices closer to those of the other major asset classes.

Disciplines served: Institutional Real Estate Investment

Membership fees: N/A

Membership requirements: N/A

Additional resources found at www.ncreif.com **:**

- Education
- Meetings
- Research
- Publications

NMHC

National Multi Housing Council

Website homepage: www.nmhc.org

Contact Information:
850 M Street, N.W. Suite 450
Washington, D.C. 20036
202-974-2300

Membership: by company
Local Chapters? no

About NMHC:
NMHC is a national association representing the interests of the nation's larger and most prominent apartment firms. NMHC advocates on behalf of rental housing, conducts apartment-related research, encourages the exchange of strategic business information, and promotes the desirability of apartment living. One-third of Americans rent their housing, and 15 percent of all U.S. households live in an apartment home.

Disciplines served: Apartment industry

Membership fees: Vary by membership type

Additional resources found at www.nmhc.org **:**

- Meetings
- Research
- Publications
- Government affairs
- Job Bank

SPONSOR

PREA

Pension Real Estate Association

Website homepage: www.prea.org

Contact Information:
100 Pearl Street, 13th Floor
Hartford, CT 06103
860-692-6341
prea@prea.org

Membership: 1300
Local Chapters? yes

About PREA:
PREA's mission is to serve its members engaged in institutional real estate investment through the sponsorship of objective forums for education, research initiatives, membership interaction and the exchange of information. The Pension Real Estate Association is a nonprofit organization whose members are engaged in the investment of tax-exempt pension and endowment funds into real estate assets. PREA is committed to providing its members with a full range of services to help develop and enhance their skills and understanding of real estate investment.

Disciplines served: anyone involved in institutional real estate

Resources: PREA plan sponsor reports, academic and research databases

Membership fees: ranges from $300 to $4900 depending on membership type

Membership requirements: application (online)

Additional resources found at: www.prea.org

Education
Meetings
Research
Publications
Government affairs
Job Bank
Scholarships

REEA

Real Estate Educators Association

Website homepage: www.reea.org

Contact Information:
19 Mantua Road
Mt. Royal, NJ 08061
856-423-3215
info@reea.org

Membership: n/a

Local Chapters? no

About REEA:
The Real Estate Educators Association is a society of professional instructors dedicated to delivering high-quality sales associates to the nation's real estate brokers, regulators and ultimately, consumers. REEA's mission is to provide resources and opportunities for professional development to individuals and organizations involved in real estate education to better serve their customer base.

Disciplines served: Real estate educators

Membership fees: $129

Membership requirements: Real estate educator or professional within discipline.

Additional resources found at: : www.reea.org

Education
Meetings
Publications
Job Bank
Scholarships

RERI

Real Estate Research Institute

Website homepage: www.reri.org

Contact Information:
100 Pearl Street, 13th Floor
Hartford, CT 06103
860-692-6341
jack@prea.org

Membership: Not a membership organization

Local Chapters? no

About RERI:
The Real Estate Research Institute is a non-profit organization created to stimulate high quality research on real estate investment performance and market fundamentals that will elevate the quality of real estate decision making. Administrative functions of the Institute are housed at the Pension Real Estate Association (PREA). The Institute's mission is to encourage research by establishing an agenda of issues critical to a better understanding of real estate markets, investment characteristics and performance; raising funds to support practical research on these key issues; funding specific proposals for research; and communicating the results as broadly as possible.

Disciplines served: Real Estate Research

Membership fees: n/a

Membership requirements: Not a membership organization. Fellows by invitation only.

Additional resources found at www.reri.org **:**

- Education
- Meetings
- Research
- Publications

RICS

Royal Institute of Chartered Surveyors

Website homepage: www.rics.org

Contact Information:
The Chrysler Building
405 Lexington Avenue Suite 2623
New York, NY 10174
917-368-8114
ricsamericas@rics.org

Membership: 110,000 worldwide

Local Chapters? no

About RICS:
The Royal Institution of Chartered Surveyors (RICS) is the leading source of land, property, and construction related knowledge. Based in Great Britain, RICS has members worldwide. The organization works to promote best practices, to represent consumers' interests, and to provide impartial advice to society, businesses, governments and global organizations. RICS Americas is the world region representing North, Central and South America, and the Caribbean. Members include property professionals engaged in building; construction; land; commercial and residential brokerage; property, project and facilities management; appraisals and real estate consulting; planning and development; and dispute resolution. RICS Americas' roles include setting high international educational and professional standards and supplying expert policy advice on property and built environment issues across the Americas.

Disciplines served: Surveyors

Membership fees: n/a

Membership requirements: Must complete RICS accredited coursework and/or meet experience and education qualifications.

Additional resources found at www.rics.org**:**

Education
Meetings
Research
Publications

SIOR

Society of Industrial and Office Realtors®

Website homepage: www.sior.com

Contact Information:
1201 New York Ave., NW, Ste. 350
Washington, DC 20005
202-449-8200
admin@sior.com

Membership: 2800
Local Chapters? yes

About SIOR:
The Society of Industrial and Office Realtors® is the leading professional commercial and industrial real estate association. The Society has certified almost 2300 of its members with the prestigious SIOR designation, a professional symbol of the highest level of knowledge, production, and ethics in the real estate industry. Real estate professionals who have earned the SIOR designation are recognized by corporate real estate executives, commercial real estate brokers and agents, lenders, and other real estate professionals as the most experienced and capable practitioners in any market. A professional affiliate of the National Association of Realtors®, the Society is dedicated to the practice and maintenance of the highest professional and ethical standards. The Society maintains a commitment to business and industry by providing outstanding professional services, publications, and educational programs.

Disciplines served: Office and Industrial specialists

Membership fees: $945 Active membership; other rates vary

Membership requirements: Must meet requirements to achieve SIOR designation; associate members must be involved in discipline.

Additional resources found at: www.sior.com

Education
Meetings
Publications
Job Bank

ULI
The Urban Land Institute
Website homepage: www.uli.org

Contact Information:
1025 Thomas Jefferson Street NW, Suite 500 West
Washington, DC 20007
202-624-7000 / 800-321-5011
reliance@uli.org

Membership: 27,000
Local Chapters? yes

About ULI:
The Urban Land Institute (ULI) is a non-profit research and education organization supported by its members. Founded in 1936, the Institute's members worldwide represent the entire spectrum of land use and real estate development disciplines, working in both private enterprise and public service. ULI facilitates the open exchange of ideas, information and experience among local, national and international industry leaders and policy makers dedicated to creating better places. The mission of the Urban Land Institute is to provide responsible leadership in the use of land to enhance the total environment.

Disciplines served: Real estate development, land use and planning

Membership fees: $325 Private sector individual; other rates vary

Membership requirements: Must be engaged within discipline

Additional resources found at www.uli.org **:**

- Education
- Meetings
- Research
- Publications
- Job Bank
- Scholarships

Part 4

Professional Profiles and Career Advice

"I always felt a need to present myself as knowledgeable, even in circumstances where I had little or no experience. I assumed that asking a question would expose my lack of expertise. I now believe just the opposite. Smart people ask questions and advance along the learning curve more rapidly.

Do not be afraid to ask questions. Knowledgeable people are generally willing to share what they have learned. Secondly, never lose the lesson from a mistake. Mistakes are inevitable and can become opportunities for those who can exercise patience and tenacity. This is easy to say and very difficult to do."

-Wayne Tiedge
CRE
Real Estate Developer
Planet Properties

Professional Profile:
Arthur Adler
Managing Director and
Chief Executive Officer,
Jones Lang LaSalle Hotels,
Americas

"There is nothing more important than just showing up and meeting people, because when you show up, you establish relationships, build rapport, and you learn how to satisfy your clients' needs."

Introduction

Arthur Adler heads the Americas division of Jones Lang LaSalle Hotels. The world's leading hotel investment services firm provides clients with value-added investment opportunities and advice, and operates 18 offices around the world.

Adler specializes in arranging hotel market transactions, financings, investment advisory services and consulting for domestic and offshore owners and investors. Adler's office is located in New York, and *Crain's New York Business Journal* previously named him as one of the top "40 under 40" business executives in New York City. The firm's parent company, Jones Lang LaSalle (NYSE: JLL), is the world's leading real estate services and investment management firm, operating across more than 100 key markets on five continents.

Education

In 1978, Adler received a Bachelor of Science degree from Cornell University in hotel management, one of the top-ranked schools for hotel management.

Career Development

After graduating from Cornell University in 1978, Adler began his career in hotel management with the idea of becoming a consultant. His first job was as an Operations Analyst at Hilton Hotels Corporation in New York. From 1980 to 1990, Adler became a Senior Principal at Laventhol & Horwath, which at the time was the leading firm providing consulting services for the hospitality industry.

"In Laventhol & Horwath, I really learned the real estate side of the business, because in addition to doing consulting related to operations, we did a lot of consulting on real estate because the firm specialized in doing market studies, financial analysis and acquisitions for hotels.

When the firm went out of business in late 1990, I became a Partner at Coopers & Lybrand in the Hospitality Consulting Group. At the time, the firm did not have a lodging consulting firm, and I was able to help the firm become one of the preeminent consulting firms in the lodging industry."

In 1998, Adler became the Managing Director of the Lodging & Leisure Group at Sonnenblick-Goldman Company, a boutique real estate investment banking firm that bought, sold, and financed hotels. Adler's diverse industry background includes consulting, litigation support, market and valuation analysis, operations and strategic planning and debt and equity transaction services to owners.

Changes Over The Years

In 2000, Adler became the Managing Director and CEO-Americas division of Jones Lang LaSalle Hotels. Adler says, *"At that time, it was the only global, fully integrated, hotels advisory business. The hotel business in general is the most global form of real estate because lenders, vendors, and brands operate globally and customers travel internationally. In arranging hotel transactions for the company, I head a business where I represent all types of owners including financial institutions, pension funds, public hotel companies, real estate investment trusts (REITs) in the sale, financing and management of major hotels. We specialize in upscale and luxury hotels and resorts. In addition, we also have a separate business that arranges transactions for select service hotels, smaller suburban hotels with limited service."*

In the US, Jones Lang LaSalle Hotels is ranked as the leading transaction advisor for hotel sales over $25 million. In 2004, its global success story includes the sale of 23,103 hotel rooms to the value of US $5.2 billion in 85 cities and advisory expertise on 132,498 rooms to the value of US $27.9 billion across 301 cities. Jones Lang LaSalle Hotels' services include transactions, mergers and acquisitions, financial advice and capital raising, valuation and appraisal, asset management, strategic planning, operator assessment and selection and industry research.

A few of Adler's clients include: InterContinental Hotels and Resorts, The Blackstone Group, Hyatt Hotels Corporation, Lend Lease, Loews, MeriStar, Starwood Hotels and Resorts, Goldman Sachs, and Prudential Insurance Company. Select assignments that Adler has overseen include a $180 million, 10-year term loan and an $80 million revolving line of credit for two properties owned by Manhattan East Suite Hotels, the $160 million sale of The Hyatt Regency Capitol Hill, a $63 million financing of the Ritz-Carlton Jamaica, the sale of Caneel Bay Resort on St. John, the $90 million sale of the Embassy Suites Chicago, a $99 million capitalization package to develop the Westin Kierland Resort in Scottsdale, Arizona, the sale of the 50 percent partnership interest in The Peabody Orlando and the operator selection process for The Diplomat Resort Country Club & Spa, the 1,060-room luxury convention hotel in Hollywood, FL.

Impact of the Internet

Adler describes how technology has made hotel transactions more efficient. "*Years ago, all materials of properties were copied in binder and shipped to clients. Today, we scan everything and post it to our secure Web site, and our investors can access all the material 24 hours a day wherever they are in the world. Furthermore, we can track when the investors obtain the documents as well as the time they take to review the documents; so we know who has done their homework."*

Personal Side

Adler is a member of the Cornell Society of Hotelmen and recently received their "Distinguished Alumni Award." He is also a member of the Urban Land Institute and is on ULI's Hotel Development Council.

His Future Business Plans

His future plans are to grow all aspects of the business at Jones Lang LaSalle Hotels. "*Specifically, we have an opportunity grow our select service hotel markets. We also want to build our active management business as well as our financing of the business. We not only sell hotels, but we bring the financing and asset management and debt financing. So we have the ability to develop many new business areas."*

Career in Corporate Real Estate

In addition to having excellent oral and written communication skills and marketing skills, he believes that his people skills have helped him succeed. "*At the end of the day, people like spending time with people they enjoy."* Adler also attributes much of his success to his formal education at Cornell: "*My education at Cornell taught me analytical skills as well as a foundation in the business. To be successful in hotels is different than all other real estate areas. You need to understand how hotels operate as a business. For example, you must learn how they are developed, financed and underwritten and which hotels compete with other properties as well as all the risks. Hotels are not like office buildings or industrial sites. If you own an office building, and you lease space to another company, they run the business in that space. In a hotel where people stay, they are the business, and people can check out like after 9/11, people checked out and didn't check in again for a while."*

Career Advice for Real Estate Professionals

For anyone wishing to build a career in the hotel industry, Arthur Adler suggests that the candidate should love to travel, enjoy the hotel industry people, and:

1. Obtain a good hotel foundation. "*A college degree in a top hotel program would not only give you a good foundation in the business, but you would build valuable relationships with people in the field."*

2. Always show up. *"And foremost in your success, I strongly believe that you must follow the words by Woody Allen in an old movie, 'half of life is showing up.' In a people-oriented business like hotels, there is nothing more important than just showing up and meeting people, because when you show up, you establish relationships, build rapport, and you learn how to satisfy your clients' needs."*

Professional Profiles:
Marshall Bennett
President
Marshall Bennett Enterprises

"You have to be in the right place at the right time. If we had built industrial parks when there was no demand, we would not have been successful."

Introduction

Marshall Bennett is President of Marshall Bennett Enterprises. He has been numbered among the most productive corporate and industrial real estate developers of the postwar period as co-founder and partner of Bennett and Kahnweiler. He is also considered to be one of the most influential people in building relationships that promote large real estate transactions in the US.

Career Development

Marshall Bennett was a pioneer in developing large industrial parks across America. Bennett began his career soon after he returned to his hometown of Chicago after serving in the Navy and pursuing his graduate education at Wharton. Impatient to get started, Bennett contacted three top business men he found listed in the "Who's Who" directory in American business. Bennett explains, "*I first went to see Mr. Scribner, head of Scribner & Company, and he sent me to Mr. Henry Isham, who referred me to Bill Hart. I ended up working for Mr. Hart, of Hart and Whetson; the firm specialized in industrial real estate. At that time Mr. Hart was the advisor to Western Electric Company and was on the board of Spiegel. In one year working for Mr. Hart, I learned more than I could have learned in several years of college."*

While having lunch with his long time friend, Louis Kahnweiler, Bennett learned about Kahnweiler's plans to open a company. "*Lou Kahnweiler told me that he wanted to open a real estate business selling factories to people who headed various companies. I immediately was intrigued and wanted to be part of it. Soon after, we formed a partnership called Bennett and Kahnweiler in 1949. In the beginning years, we bought pieces of vacant land with other financial partners, and we developed them for industrial use and then, leased the properties."* Bennett and Kahnweiler is one of Chicago's oldest corporate real estate firms with broad-based expertise in industrial and office brokerage, development, investment and consulting. Bennett was the developer.

In 1954, Bennett and Kahnweiler developed their first comprehensive planned industrial district, the O'Hare Industrial Park. While looking for more land in the area, Bennett discovered the Centex (for Central Texas) Construction Company. "*I was immediately interested in the possibilities of bridging the two-mile area between the planned residential development and the new O'Hare airport, because Centex had a terrific piece of property for an industrial park. We brought together Chicago's Pritzker family with the Texas-based Murchison brothers to make the deal happen.*" Bennett was able to bring the parties together because he had been childhood friends with Jay Pritzker, the eldest of the three sons of Chicago businessman Abram Nicholas ("A. N.") Pritzker and Jay had backed him in a number of deals. *"We first found a property West of O'Hare field owned by Centex, and I convinced Clint Murchinson that we had some pretty good partners with the Pritzkers. During the deal, I had many anxious calls from A.N. Pritzker, because he was not as confident in the deal as I portrayed that I was. Before Centex, the biggest development I had done was 40 acres. Here we started with over 675, but I believed that our vision for the property was perfect with the future expansion of O'Hare airport and the surrounding area."* Because of Bennett and Kahnweiler's vision and perseverance, the company pioneered the field of industrial development by creating the 2,200 acre Centex Industrial Park in Elk Grove Village in 1957 through 1973. The success of Centex helped spur the real estate development boom in the northwest suburbs.

Changes Over The Years

With the success of Centex, the firm expanded to develop state-of-the-art industrial and office parks in major cities across the country. *"Phil Klutznick then asked us to help him developed Montbello in Denver. Montbello, at the edge of Denver's then airport, was our first move out of Chicago; the airport is Stapleton Field now being developed as a community by Albert Ratner of Forest City Enterprises. We sold Montbello out in record time-- five and a half years, because the market in Denver was just coming into its own in the early 1970s."* At the time, the Park was billed as "Tomorrow's Industrial Park...Today", and it still remains an integral part of the community. During the course of the decade, Bennett & Kahnweiler developed more than 71 buildings with square footage in excess of four million square feet on over 600 acres in Denver.

"From Montbello, we kept on building industrial parks." Bennett and Kahnweiler went on to develop over 26 state-of-the-art industrial and office parks in Denver, St. Louis, Milwaukee, San Francisco, Atlanta, Southern California, as well as many other major sites in Chicago. In 1979, Bennett was named "Man of the Year by the National Association of Industrial and Office Properties.

In 1977, Bennett's life took an unexpected turn when he suffered a severe head injury as a result of a kayak accident in Idaho. *"This accident changed the direction of my business decisions. As soon as I fully recovered in 1982, I launched a new business, Marshall Bennett Enterprises.*

Since then, I have been involved in many diverse business ventures." He formed a Chicago-based joint venture, Miller-Klutznick Davis Gray/Bennett Co. He later invested to help Goldie Wolf, a fantastic commercial Realtor, open her own real estate company.

Education

Bennett received his BA degree from University of Chicago. He then attended the Wharton School of Business and Finance in Philadelphia for a year in the M.B.A. Program. And later, he attended graduate studies at the University of Chicago.

Personal Side

Bennett has received numerous awards, including the Chicago Urban Land Institute Lifetime Achievement Award and the Hall of Fame Award from the Chicago Association of Realtors. He serves on the Board of Governors of the University of Chicago Hospitals, Board of Directors, Evanston Hospital, Trustee of Chicago Symphony Orchestral, and The Weizmann Institute in Israel, The "Think Tank" and The EastWest Institute.

In addition, he gives much of his time towards building the Chicago School of Real Estate at Roosevelt University with his friend and co-founder, Gerald Fogelson. *"Most people become involved in real estate transactions during their lifetime, and I wanted to give students the opportunity to learn about real estate investments and ownership. This is a wonderful pragmatic program."*

Career Advice for Real Estate Professionals

Bennett believes in four guiding principles:

1. Have Fun. *"You must first find an area where you can have fun while working."*

2. Real Estate Education is Important. "*Today, there are many terrific real estate programs such as Roosevelt's or Wharton's program where you get a hands-on, pragmatic,*

education that will help you succeed in business."
3. Timing is Everything. *"You have to be in the right place at the right time. If we had built industrial parks when there was no demand, we would not have been successful."*
4. Treat Others Fairly. "*If you want to succeed, you should not try to outsmart others. Instead you must protect your professional reputation and always do right by people."*

Professional Profiles:
Gerald W. Fogelson
Founder and President
Fogelson Companies
Co-chairman and CEO
Central Station Development Corporation

"You should always look at your next opportunity and challenge yourself---it makes working fun each and everyday."

Introduction

During his career, Fogelson has completed billions of dollars in almost every type of real-estate transaction as a developer throughout Indiana, Illinois, Wisconsin, Ohio, New Jersey, Florida, Kentucky and California. His career includes single-family attached and detached residential housing, garden and high-rise apartments, shopping centers, office buildings, condominiums, townhouses, mid-rise and high-rise developments, themed communities, marinas, mezzanine and equity financing, land development, adaptive reuse, industrial parks and mixed-use. He pioneered the Planned Unit Development in the early 1960s and was a leader in mixed developments. Currently, Mr. Fogelson is developing Central Station with a joint venture with Albert Ratner of Forest City Enterprises, an 80-acre, $3-billion mixed-use development in downtown Chicago. This is not only the largest planned development in Chicago, but one of the largest in the country.

Education

In 1955, Fogelson graduated cum laude from Lehigh University in Bethlehem, Pennsylvania in Business

Administration with a major in marketing. He then attended night school at Rutgers University in New Jersey to learn how to read plans.

Career Development

Fogelson was born in Dover, New Jersey, where his father owned and operated a small shoe store. *"When I graduated, my father thought that since I was the first in my family to graduate college, I could be successful at anything He knew a friend who was successful at building homes, so he lent me the money to buy two lots to build houses. I then started Thor-Built Homes Inc., a small company that built single family homes in New Jersey. The first homes I built were priced from $9,900, including the lot. In June, 1955, I formed Fogelson Development Company.* In the next two years, he built free-standing homes and subdivisions, becoming one of the most active builders in Morris County.

In 1958, after serving in the Army for two years, Fogelson broke ground on the Highland Merchandise Mart, in Indiana, which became the forerunner of the discount department store era. In 1961, Fogelson relocated to Indianapolis, Indiana. There, his Development Company began building single family subdivisions and garden apartment projects. For the next seven years, he built throughout Indiana, Illinois, Ohio and Kentucky. In 1968, Fogelson formed a joint-venture with the Norfolk and Western Railroad to develop Briar East, one of the largest apartment/commercial properties in Indiana. Also in conjunction with the railroad, he developed a project in Ohio. He later bought out the railroad and continued to own and operate the properties for years.

In the seventies, Fogelson developed apartments, single family residential projects and commercial properties in Indiana including Tiberon Trails in Merrillville and Pine Island Ridge in Lake County, Indiana. Pine Island utilized almost 500 acres to create apartments, housing, shopping, offices, town homes, four man-made lakes and more. Pine Island was, at that time, the largest development done in Lake County. He also opened an office in Florida and developed properties in the state. Fogelson says, "*I subsequently purchased properties in various cities, and got them entitled, constructing streets and infrastructure and selling the finished lots to both public and private home builders in Illinois and Indiana. At the same time, I became interested in adaptive re-use of existing buildings.*" Fogelson purchased and rebuilt the Patterson-McCormick Mansion and the Wrigley Office Mansion in Chicago, a former cold storage warehouse in Milwaukee, and The Weibod building in Chicago called West Town.

In 1986, Fogelson purchased the estate of Douglas Stewart, the founder of Quaker Oats, and developed the equestrian themed community known as Hunt Club Farms. Fogelson's work also included the restoration of the former S&H building into a modern industrial park, and the construction of marinas and dinner boats in Wisconsin.

Changes Over The Years

In 1988, Fogelson entered into a contract to purchase the property owned by the Illinois Central Railroad at Roosevelt Road and Michigan Avenue in Chicago. Today, this project is an 80 acre $3.5 billion development known as Central Station; it is Chicago's largest mixed-use development and when completed, will contain almost 7000 condominiums, townhouses and apartments, along with retail, hotel and office properties. Central Station is now considered to be the catalyst that empowered and moved the growth of the near south side of Chicago. Fogelson describes Central Station,

"*The first day I looked at the property, I was amazed. On the north border of the property is Grant Park. Our entire east border is Lake Shore Drive, the Museum Campus and Soldier Field. Our entire south border is McCormick Place, the world's largest convention center. And our west border is Michigan Avenue. So in the midst of all this world-renowned infrastructure, we were the undeveloped hole in the middle of the doughnut. My attorney and friend Leonard Schanfield told me that this would be a once-in-a-lifetime opportunity to test everything I had ever known, and that if I was successful, I would leave a legacy behind me that my children, my grandchildren and people in Chicago would be able to enjoy for years to come. I had such respect for him, that I embraced his vision. He was dying of cancer, and I agreed to do it if he would work with me side by side. Leonard's final gift was to introduce me to one of the truly great companies and one of the true visionaries in American real estate, Albert Ratner of Forest City Enterprises. Central Station was a crossroads in my life. There would have been no other project that I would have encountered that would have extended me on such a personal and business basis. And as a result of my success, I can't wait to come to work 365 days a year and continue to challenge myself.*"

Recently, Central Station: The Realization of a Dream was published. In his own words, Fogelson describes how the property evolved as a successful development in downtown Chicago. In 2002, the Chicago City Council honored him for his prominence as developer and for creating the Chicago School of Real Estate.

Personal Side

Fogelson is a strong advocate of "giving back." Along with Marshall Bennett, Fogelson co-founded the Chicago School of Real Estate at Roosevelt University and serves a co-chair of the Advisory Council. Fogelson was the first endowed real-estate chair at Roosevelt University, and the Gerald W. Fogelson Chair is now occupied by Jon Devries. He also started the Fogelson Forum at Roosevelt. He explains, *"After my success in real estate, I wanted to make it possible for younger people to have access and perhaps get involved in real estate. The mission of The Chicago School is to raise the quality of education for professionals, create career opportunities and enhance the industry through a diversified, pragmatic program.*" Fogelson serves on numerous boards including: Mount Sinai Hospital, Near South Planning

Board, and Valley Partners at California State University.

Career in Corporate Real Estate

Fogelson credits his success to his entrepreneurial leadership style: "*I have always had the ability to find experts with whom I can outsource work or do joint ventures. I characterize our operations as being more like a combat squad than a battalion. I like action, and I believe in seizing the opportunity. I only take time to reflect when I travel.*"

Career Advice for Real Estate Professionals

Fogelson suggests that you embrace three concepts to be successful in real estate:

1. Look at the Big Picture. "*You should think like a business person and deal with each and every decision in a holistic sense so you can measure and evaluate the risks and the rewards of all of the disciplines of the business, such as construction verses marketing verses finance from that business basis.*"

2. Get a formal education. "*Today, entry to most professions usually requires solid education and training in the specific field. A university education teaches you to think, gives you perspective, and hopefully, like the Chicago School of Real Estate, you also get a practical education, internships and network with people in your area of expertise.*"

3. Challenge yourself. "*As Central Station challenged me, you should always look at your next opportunity and challenge yourself---it makes working fun each and everyday.*"

Professional Profiles:

E. Rene Frank

Chairman
Global Housing Foundation
in partnership with
the United Nations

"I believe that professionalism requires you to have an education, a license, and handle yourself in a very professional manner."

Introduction

E. Rene Frank is President of the Global Housing Foundation in partnership with the UN-Habitat located in New York. In this capacity, he clears slums in major cites and builds affordable housing worldwide. Frank has been actively engaged in various aspects of the real estate profession and real estate education since 1952. He was the first well-known international broker of large real estate portfolios. He was a partner of Jean-Marc Levet & Partners, the President of Properties at Auction, and the chairman of International Property Counselors, Ltd. and Panorama International, Ltd. He is an Honorary World President, International Real Estate Federation (FIABCI).

Education

Frank received a Bachlor's degree from Aixen Provence in France, where he had also attended law school. He received a real estate salesman's license in NY in 1950, and he joined the New York Real Estate Board in 1952. He attended real estate courses at Columbia University, and passed his broker's license in '53. Frank explains, *"I have always been very interested in real estate education, because I felt that it is the basis of our 'profession.' In 1983, I started the Certified International Property Specialists (CIPS) program for the National Associaton of Realtors (NAR).* " Frank also taught the first International Real Estate course at New York University in 1974. Since then, he has helped many universities develop international real estate programs. Today, he is working for the International Federation of Real Esate Professionals (FIABCI) to help them create International Real Estate Diplomas, in conjunction with FIABCI approved Universities.

Career Development

Frank came to the United States from France in 1948 and stayed because he met his future wife. He needed a job, and the only job he could find listed in the New York Times was to sell real estate on weekends for *Ruland & Benjamin.* After one year working for them, he read in the papers that the remaining heir to the Fish family portofilio had died. "*My firm managed a huge portfolio of Mr. Stuyvesant's family, who was the last living heir of the first Dutch settlers in New York. I convinced the president of my firm that we should get a mandate to sell the entire portfolio, consisting of about 108 properties in Manhattan. All of our major clients in NY declined as the properties were located in marginal areas of Manhattan. So during a trip to Paris to visit my family, I met a banker and through the banker, I met a French real estate investor. And the real estate investor came over to New York and within two weeks, he decided to make an offer for the whole package in the millions of dollars. This was a major transaction that hit the first page in the New York Times and was covered on TV. That deal started me off in the big league of emerging Inernational Real Estate Transactions, and also convinced me that there was an unexplored niche of our Real Estate Market called: International Real Estate.*"

Changes Over The Years

In 1957, Frank started his own company by advertising in the New York Times, 'E. Rene Frank International Real

Estate Company; International Real Estate Exclusively.' Frank explains, *"People were laughing at me. They said, 'Isn't there enough work in this country?' In the 50s, it was equivalent to a veterinary advertising his specially was dinosaurs."* Frank completed many major assignments. Frank says, "*For example, the World Trade Center appointed my firm in 1967 as its European representative for leasing space in the World Trade Center which we did that very successfully with major banks and some other European clients. Also, I had several assignments overseas: Through my friendship with the founder and chairman of Holiday Inns, Mr. Kemmons Wilson, I became a consultant and agent for sites for Holiday Inn to expand in Holland, Germany, France and Spain. I also became the consultant to the then Chemical Bank and to the U.S. State Department. They had several large portfolios.*"

In 1965, Frank started opening offices overseas. His first overseas office was established in Paris, France. "*We were entrusted to make a survey for all properties owned by the U.S. government in France. Our second office was in Spain, where we handled assignments for US firms such as Armstrong of Lancaster PA, Xerox, Swift in Chicago, now called Beatrice Foods and many others,*" says Frank. He continued to open eight affiliated offices in various parts of the world. And in 1995, he sold the company to Mr. Jean-Marc Levet of Levet & Partners.

Then, Rene Frank turned his attention to building homes for the poor. "*I had been FIABCI's representative to the U.N. since the 70's. After I visited Managua, Nicaragua as Honorary Deputy President of FIABCI, I was struck by the appalling poverty of its people, especially in terms of housing. As a real estate professional, I was convinced that there should be a way to remedy the situation. In my capacity as FIABCI's permanent representative to the UN, I took advantage of a UN-Habitat meeting in Nairobi, Kenya and launched the GLOBAL HOUSING FOUNDATION, with the explicit purpose of helping the poor to obtain decent housing, and to improve slums and shantytowns." Shortly after that meeting, the Foundation tackled its first project, providing assistance to the residents of the "Dieciocho de Mayo" (Eighteenth of May) a shantytown in Managua, a labyrinth of over 900 hovels, housing some 4.000 people. Rather than giving away housing, the basic principle was to sell new homes at a price affordable enough without interest payments to make them accessible to the poorest purchaser."* Mr. Rene Frank has received several awards for his work with providing homeownership for slum dwellers across the globe including: In 2004, FIABCI created the Rene Frank Award to permanently link his name with the yearly Award. In 2002, he received the medal of Valor from Prince Philippe of Belgium. Also, in 2002 he was appointed a member of The U.N. Task Force No. 8, dealing with world-wide conditions of slum dwellers.

Personal Side

Today, Rene Frank spends most of his time building housing for the poor and designing international real estate education programs. He is also a moderator and guest speaker at conventions around the world on these topics. He is often quoted from his work as the author of several books and articles including '100 Cities', a professional textbook; Rent Control: Its Conditions and Effects in 85 Countries. In addition, because of his role as consultant to officials on policy issues pertaining to real estate, development and foreign property issues, his views have appeared in the U.S. Congressional Record.

Career in Corporate Real Estate

In addition to finding his niche, Rene Frank attributes his success in the international arena to the fact that he understands the importance that culture plays in business decisions, he speaks five languages, and he has had the patience to build the business.

Career Advice for Real Estate Professionals

Frank offers several suggestions to real estate professionals who want to succeed in the international business arena:

1. Be educated. "*You have to have the basic skills and knowledge of the field. Today, it is much, much easier to do business with foreign clients, particularly when the basic commodity – namely real estate is translated to global values.*"

2. Understand culture. "*It would help for you to know all the factors that respect the cultures of the people you are dealing with, including speaking several languages and being patient and not too pushy in your business relationships.*"

3. Act professional. "*I believe that professionalism requires you to have an education, a license, and handle yourself in a very professional manner.*"

4. Join organizations. "*You should belong to prestigious real estate associations which specialize in the field and can provide you with valuable contacts.*"

Professional Profiles:
Steven L. Good
Chairman & CEO,
Sheldon Good & Company

"It is very important to develop a résumé that distinguishes you from everyone else. The number one question that always ran through my head is 'Why should someone choose you?'"

Introduction

Attorney Steven L. Good is Chairman and Chief Executive Officer of Sheldon Good & Company, which has been ranked as the largest firm in the United States exclusively conducting real estate auctions. The company was also previously ranked as the sixth largest commercial brokerage firm in the United States. Good has been the driving force in the recent expansion of the company. The company has sold over $8 billion of real estate including commercial, office, retail, industrial, residential, and vacant land sites. The company was founded in 1965 by Good's father, Sheldon Good; the company's corporate office is located in Chicago, Illinois.

Education

Good earned his Bachelor of Science in Finance (magna cum laude) from Syracuse University and a Juris Doctor from DePaul University College of Law. He is an Accredited Auctioneer of Real Estate (AARE), Auction Marketing Institute. Good says, *"I believe that education is a cornerstone of a good career. I continue to keep up my own credentials. In addition, I have worked for the past several years to help students learn, especially about careers in real estate for Mayor's Daley's 'Principal For A Day Program' (PFAD) and at Robert Morris College."* Good received an honorary Doctor of Humane Letters from Robert Morris in 1999 for his work with students.

Career Development

Prior to joining Sheldon Good & Company, Good took several internships and jobs as a way to broaden his experiences, develop his network, and build his résumé. Good worked for the United States Senate in Washington, D.C.; the Cook County, Illinois Assessor's Office; the Building, Code and Zoning Division of the Cook County, State Attorney's Office; and the U.S. Department of Justice, Office of the U.S. Attorney, District of Columbia. "*I learned from these experiences that I did not want to become a practicing lawyer. And in 1980, I took a summer job working for my father at Sheldon Good & Company, and I loved the business from the beginning. I sold a big building and made an enormous commission. Immediately, this moved me to the transaction side of the business, and I wanted to be in the brokerage business and build our auction business, which was only a small part of our company at that time. Because of my educational and business background, I thought that auctions made a lot of sense for many different reasons: Years ago, real estate auctions were used as a last resort for properties that were not easily valued. But, I have always believed that with turbulent and uncertain market conditions, auctions provide property owners often better solutions than selling their properties in the traditional manner. At that time, we had no competitors and no prototype, and most of the people working in the field didn't want to be selling properties at auction. But, I had confidence that we were doing something unique, and because of that I have been a very good advocate for our company by never being afraid to ask for business. Because of my strong beliefs, our company had a wider reach and attained a greater volume than anyone else in the industry"* adds Good. Because of his confidence, Good has been a guest speaker at many conferences including: The National Association of REALTORS® Convention, The Chicago Bar Association, The Urban Development Forum at Harvard University, The REALTORS® Land Institute (RLI), and the Fogelson Forum.

Changes Over The Years

Since taking the leadership reins of the company in 1987, Good has helped the company grow dramatically. In the summer of 2001, Good completed the purchase of Sheldon Good & Company International and its subsidiaries from his father, Sheldon Good. As a result of the sale, a corporate partnership was established so that its people could share in the company's profits. At the age of 44, Good became the Chairman and CEO of Sheldon Good & Company International, LLC. This partnership was designed to retain and attract the best talent, which positioned the Company for revolutionary growth. *"Recently, we expanded our business in many ways including the number of people in the firm, the types of projects we handle, and the geography we cover. We now cover over seventy classes of real estate located throughout the world. Today, our company is to the real estate business what Sotheby's or Christie's is to the fine art and collectibles business."*

Impact of the Internet

With new technologies, Good has been able to build a more efficient business model, and he is able to maintain his license in several states by taking continuing education courses online, often in his pajamas. Good currently is licensed by reciprocity in many states.

Personal Side

Although running the company takes up much of his time, he loves writing about the business in his free time, and he is widely published as an authority in the auction industry such as: *The Real Estate Review, Real Estate Business Magazine, Real Estate Today* and *The Corporate Real Estate Leader.* He currently has a multi-book deal with Dearborn Trade Publishing. His first book for Dearborn, *Churches, Jails, and Gold Mines...Mega-Deals from a Real Estate Maverick* became a best seller in 2003. Good explains, "*We have so much fun doing business that I love writing about some of the most unusual and high stakes deals that the Company has been involved in. My first book chronicles some of our recent deals such as a jail in Indiana, Michael Jordan's restaurant building in Chicago, gold mines in Montana, art deco hotels in South Beach, and Trump Plaza of Palm Beach, Florida. I love writing in my free time, because it helps me clarify my thoughts, get deeper insight, and the publications help me build my reputation and brand name in the field.*"

In addition to all his other activities, Good has been involved in many philanthropic endeavors. He was the 2004 president of the Chicago Association of REALTORS®, a 12,000 member association. At the same time, he was also the Chairman of the National Auction Forum for the National Association of REALTORS®. He has received numerous honors for his service including he was a past recipient of the DePaul University College of Law Alumni Service Award.

His Future Business Plans

Good continues to expand Sheldon Good & Company worldwide. With virtually no competitors, he has several business goals for the future growth of the Company: "*I first want to continue to develop talent. I have always believed that our top people were not easily replaceable. Our people have become even more critical to our success as we have expanded, because the business has gotten more complex. So, the key to growing our business is growing people who can tell our story, service our clients and then building an infrastructure that can service the business. In*

2004, I raised $250 million to advance funds for the sale of real estate at auctions. I plan to continue to expand our lending business as well as our conventional brokerage capabilities by creating a family of companies that can serve all our clients and our brokerage affiliations" Good says.

Career in Corporate Real Estate

Apart from the analytical skills he gained from his formal education, Good thinks that hard work, professionalism, networking, and most importantly, being known for doing a complete job have helped him succeed. *"I believe in the philosophy that 'you can count on me' attitude. Whatever assignment I accept, whether it is paid or in a volunteer position, once I am given an opportunity, I do a professional job. For example, I have built many terrific business relationships through my associations with DePaul. I chose DePaul Law School because it had such a strong history of developing well-connected people in Chicago. Better than 95 percent of the graduates from DePaul Law School stay in greater Chicago. Through experience, I have learned that deals come and go, but relationships carry the day. The real estate business is very much a 'who you know' business, especially as more businesses are becoming global."*

Career Advice for Real Estate Professionals

Good offers several key strategies for building your career in corporate real estate:

1. Explore career opportunities. *"You should be exposed to many different kinds of jobs through internships and part-time jobs so that you find out what you love to do; what you do not like to do, and what fits your talents both ethically and professionally.*

2. Develop your niche. "*It is very important to develop a résumé that distinguishes you from everyone else. The number one question that always ran through my head is*

'Why should someone choose you?'"

3. Education is important. *"You have to be able to read, write, and count, and many times you must have the ability to do all three at one time."*

4. Do a professional job. *"Ultimately, once you have the job, then you must walk through that door and use the opportunity to do a complete job both professionally and ethically, because your reputation will lead you to new career opportunities."*

5. Build your network. *"Last and most important, you should find areas where you have the opportunity to expand your network. Better than a third of the people we do business with are people with whom we already have some connection. And, if anybody in our company gets into a jam, we know how to pick up a phone and help each other. And that is really what business relationships are all about. Nobody is bullet-proof. If someone can recommend you in your field, you will have a leg up on others. I have learned that nobody succeeds on his or her own. There is no such thing as a totally self-made person. The Beatles got it right, 'You get by with a little help from your friends'"* concludes Good.

Professional Profiles:
Daniel L. Goodwin
Chairman and CEO
The Inland Real Estate
Group of Companies

"You need to have both persistence and perseverance. You must work hard continually to be successful."

Introduction

Daniel L. Goodwin is Chairman and CEO of The Inland Real Estate Group of Companies, Inc. The Inland Real Estate Group of Companies, Inc. is comprised of independent real estate investment and financial companies, with managed assets in excess of $10 billion, doing business nationwide with a strong presence in over 41 states with corporate headquarters in Illinois. Inland is one of the nation's largest commercial real estate companies with over 35 years experience in real estate investment, commercial real estate brokerage, land development, construction, and mortgage lending. Inland is regarded as:

- 5th Largest Property Manager in the United States
- 3rd Fastest Acquirer of Retail Property in the United States
- The Top Retail Owner in Atlanta
- 16th Biggest Financial Intermediary in the United States
- 5th Largest Shopping Center owner in the United States.
- Sponsored 3 Real Estate Investment Trust (REITS), one is the 2nd Largest in Chicagoland.
- Recognized for Affordable Housing Developments

Education

Mr. Goodwin obtained his Bachelor's Degree from Northeastern Illinois University in 1966, and his Master's Degree at Northern Illinois in education in 1971.

Career Development

Growing up, Goodwin was always fascinated by both education and real estate. Goodwin first chose to be a teacher. Goodwin explains. "*In high school, I decided that I wanted to be a teacher. After I earned my BA, I continued at night school to receive two state certified qualifications in teaching. I taught school for five years, primarily 7th and 8th grade science for May School in the Chicago Public School System, and I really enjoyed it.*"

Mr. Goodwin has been in the housing industry for over 35 years. He describes how he entered real estate, "*In 1967, I suggested to three teachers that I had known from teaching, two of them went to school with me at Northeastern and one of them I met when I began teaching, that we should put our money together and buy an apartment building. And the only thing we could afford was a three flat not far from May School. Next, I got other teachers to invest their money with us. Our business continued to grow as many other teachers heard about what we were doing. In 1968, we were making money; so we decided to incorporate Inland Real Estate Corporation. And at that time, I was teaching during the day, working real estate at nights and on weekends and going to graduate school the other nights. By the time I had finished my master's degree, we had built up so much equity in the real estate, and we had hired people, so it became a point where I had to devote more and more time to real estate, which meant I eventually had to make a hard choice to leave teaching to work full-time in the real estate business.*"

Goodwin's companies continued to expand its operations

in Florida, Arizona, and New England. Goodwin says, *"As we expanded nationally, there were three major obstacles that we faced; in our early years, our main obstacle was really a question of financial survival until the business became profitable. The second biggest challenge was to deal with changes in the business such as tax reform in the 80's, and still remain profitable. We gained an outstanding reputation in the industry because of our ability to make money. Our third challenge was learning how to deal with different types of investors. Our early investors were teachers at May School who were very hands on; they would look at the properties. Because of our reputation for making money, by the mid-70s, we were attracting more and more passive investors."*

Changes Over The Years

Today, Daniel Goodwin heads over twelve major corporations as part of the Inland Group of Companies. In 2004, Inland sponsored three Real Estate Investment Trusts (REITs): Inland Real Estate Corp., which owns and manages 140 retail properties in eight states and more than $1.2 billion in assets; Inland Retail Real Estate Trust Inc., which oversees more than 270 retail properties primarily east of the Mississippi River and more than $4.4 billion in assets; and Inland Western Retail Real Estate Trust Inc. which began acquiring retail properties west of the Mississippi River in October 2003 and has a portfolio of more than 60 properties. Goodwin adds, *"When we offered the first of three REITs that Inland has sponsored, the biggest change was the significant amount of time executives had to take away from running the business to focus on setting up guidelines and procedures to document everything in order to eliminate opportunities for fraud. But ultimately, it will be extremely beneficial not just for the shareholders of these companies, but also for the people in the companies, because they have better control, and we have been very profitable."*

Personal Side

Goodwin believes that to stay healthy to do the business, he must exercise, eat correctly, and pace himself. He enjoys fishing, hiking and boating, and occasionally bowling and playing golf.

Goodwin adds, *"I use many of my real estate skills to help with many educational pursuits."* Mr. Goodwin is currently Vice Chairman of the Board of Trustees of Benedictine University and Springfield College and Chairman of the Board of Northeastern Illinois University. Goodwin instituted a program to educate disabled students about the workplace. Most of those original students are employed at Inland today, and Inland continues as one of the largest employers of the disabled in DuPage County. He has won numerous awards including: Outstanding Trustee of the Decade Award *Northeastern Illinois University* – Honorary Doctorate and President's Meritorious Service Award. He is also the co-author of a nationally recognized real estate reference book for the management of residential properties titled: *The Landlord's Handbook* published by Dearborn Trade Publishing.

His Future Business Plans

Goodwin plans to continue to expand the Inland Group of Companies. He also spends a great deal of his time meeting with heads of each company regularly. Goodwin adds, *"Inland has been an incubator of real estate companies for more than 30 years. We have developed and nurtured companies following our own unique business model. We are proud of our accomplishments and we believe our best years lie ahead."*

Career in Corporate Real Estate

Goodwin attributes much of his success to his educational background, love of learning, understanding financial aspects of the business, and most importantly, his leadership qualities of inspiring others to succeed. *"I believe as a leader in being positive and talking health, happiness and prosperity to every person I meet. I spend a lot of my day working with the young executives and employees to help them succeed in my organization."*

Career Advice for Real Estate Professionals

Goodwin says, *"I believe to be successful in real estate, you need four things:*

1. **Get a good education.** *"If you want a career in the commercial real estate business, it really is important to have a good educational background. Our recruiters concentrate on hiring educated people at job fairs in their local markets."*

2. **Have passion for the field.** *"When you start in the business, you should quickly determine if you love the real estate business and try to find your niche in it."*

3. **Be Persistent.** *"You need to have both persistence and perseverance. You must work hard continually to be successful."*

4. **Have Patience.** *"If you follow the guidelines above, and you are moderately talented and you are patient, you have a very good chance of success. I have found by experience that rarely do people get rich quickly. Your wealthy real estate people generally have built their success gradually after many years in the business."*

Professional Profiles: Peter Linneman

Albert Sussman Professor of Real Estate, Finance, and Public Policy at the Wharton School of Business

"Relationships are essential to your success in business and life. Even for a 'numbers' person, it's all about people."

Introduction

A member of Wharton's faculty since 1979, Dr. Peter Linneman served as the founding chairman of Wharton's Real Estate Department, and was the Director of Wharton's Zell-Lurie Real Estate Center. A highly sought-after speaker, Linneman is widely recognized as one of the leading strategic thinkers in the real estate industry, and was recently named one of the 25 most influential people in real estate by Realtor Magazine.

Education

Dr. Linneman holds a BA from Ashland College in 1973, an MA from University of Chicago in 1976, and a Ph.D. from the University of Chicago in 1977, where he was also a Post Doctoral Fellow in Economics of the University of Chicago in 1977.

Career Development

Early in his college years at Ashland College, Lucille Ford, his professor, suggested he use his talents to teach. Linneman says, *"I really liked economics from the first day I took the course with Lucille Ford, and Lucille and two other faculty members suggested that I had a certain degree of aptitude for it and should attend graduate school. So I applied and was accepted at University of Chicago. Several professors at the University helped me do research and start teaching at the University: Milton Friedman, George Stigler, Ted Schultz, Gary Becker, George Tolley and Jim Heckman. Many of these professors went on to win a Nobel Prize.* In 1978, Linneman became the Assistant Professor of Business Economics at the Graduate School of Business at the University of Chicago.

From 1979 through 1984, Linneman was the Assistant Professor of Finance and Public Policy at Wharton School of the University of Pennsylvania. His teaching and research focused on real estate and investment strategies, mergers and acquisitions, and international markets. In 1984, Linneman became an Associate Professor and in 1988 was appointed as Professor of Finance and Public Policy at Wharton. In 1989, he was named the Albert Sussman Professor of Real Estate, Professor of Finance and Public Policy and Management at the Samuel Zell and Robert Lurie Real Estate Center at Wharton, where he was the Director of the Center from 1985 through 1998. He was appointed Chairperson, Wharton Real Estate Department from 1994-1997. The Wharton program is regularly identified as a top program in real estate, and Linneman is credited as a major contributor to the program's success.

Changes Over The Years

In 1978, Dr. Linneman formed Linneman Associates, a consulting firm located in Pennsylvania. Linneman says, "*Almost immediately after I started teaching, through recommendations, I began consulting as a sideline for Michelin Tire Company and Scott Paper. Both my consulting practice and my teaching career have prospered ever since. Consulting gave my academic life a balance and added to me being a better teacher.*" When Linneman began his practice, he mainly consulted on antitrust litigation. Today, he advises global companies in real estate finance and investments, general business strategy, financial analysis, and human strategy. At universities, he has also been involved in the creation of real estate programs where he has consulted in all areas such as the development of programs, design of curriculum, hiring of staff, acquiring students and marketing of the programs. His clients have included: Lubert-Adler Investments, Equity International Properties, Sunbelt Management, GMAC, Michelin Tire, IBM, General Electric Capital Corporation, Paramount Group, and Roosevelt University.

In addition to teaching and consulting, Linneman has been very successful as a practitioner. During a one-year leave from Wharton he served as Senior Managing Director of Equity International Properties LLC, a global real estate investment firm. "*I worked with Sam Zell to help him establish Equity International LLC. I learned a lot from flying with Sam Zell for fourteen months all over the world. My involvement as a practitioner always occurred when I had a consulting assignment and through the circumstances of my consulting, it resulted in me becoming a practitioner, and I always enjoyed it because it gave me action, access to leaders and new ideas, and it helped me to be a much better teacher.*" Linneman served as Vice Chairman of Amerimar Realty, and was Chairman of the Board of Rockefeller Center Properties Trust. In this latter capacity he led the process of foreclosing on its Japanese owners and the successful sale of Rockefeller Center. He has served and continues to serve on the board of directors of numerous NYSE and private companies. Dr. Linneman is the founder and Principal of the American Growth Land Fund, a $100 million investment vehicle that invests in long term land developments in high growth areas of the US. He is a partner in Gerber-Taylor Realty Fund III, a real estate fund-of-funds.

Linneman is a noted speaker and moderator for leading corporations and professional associations around the world. *"I started speaking to bring attention to Wharton's program. Later on, I was asked to moderate several conferences. For example, for the past 14 years I have been a co-coordinator/sponsor/moderator with Sam Zell of a prestigious real estate roundtable conference by invitation only each year that brings in very high level people, called "The Marshall Bennett Classic."*

Since the beginning of his teaching career, Dr. Linneman has written for over 70 publications. He is the founding co-editor of *The Wharton Real Estate Review.* He publishes a quarterly newsletter *The Linneman Letter*, a leading economic and real estate strategy research publication that claims more than 120 leading real estate firms as subscribers. In 2001, he wrote a real estate textbook, *Real Estate Finance and Investments: Risks and Opportunities*, which has been adopted at leading universities, including Yale, John Hopkins, USC, Brown, Columbia, and Wharton, and has quickly become the leading reference source for those interested in real estate finance and investment. "*I always hoped that leaders would want to read and could understand what I wrote, and I am fortunate to have achieved this goal. Writing is very rewarding.*"

Personal side

Among the skills that enable Linneman to be effective are his devotion to hard work and to continually learning new material, his ability to see the 'big picture" and to cultivate a network of people. "*I view much of my success as attributable to building lasting relationships with many people such as with Lucille Ford, Sam Zell, Albert Behler, and Marshall Bennett, and growing through these relationships*" adds Linneman.

His Future Business Plans

Teaching has allowed Dr. Linneman to have the independence and control to build many other successful business paths. In the next five years, he plans to continue to teach at Wharton, build new business ventures, and take time to travel with family members. And most importantly, he wants to continue to have fun whether working or playing.

Career Advice for Real Estate Professionals

Linneman says there are several important strategies you need to have to be successful:

1. **Find out early your talents:** "*The sooner you can figure out what you love and what you are extraordinary at, the better you can make the most of your talents.*"

2. **Continue to Learn:** "*It is just too competitive if you are not open to continually learning through a wide range of resources including talking with people in variety of circles, reading in a wide range of fields, learning new technologies, and getting a formal education. Today, a formal education gives you credentials, helps you gain analytical and research skills and you learn without making as many costly mistakes. Education is like going to a batting cage. You learn by practicing how to do things better, and you are not punished for making mistakes. Today, there are many good real estate programs, so you are at a disadvantage without that education in the job market.*"

3. **Build Relationships**: "*Relationships are essential to your success in business and life. Even for a 'numbers' person, it's all about people.*"

4. **A good career should be a journey, not a destination:** "*I mentor many students on how to achieve success in their careers. Students always want their success to happen overnight. But I have learned that building a career is more about the journey and building relationships than overnight success. Career success is like playing basketball. When you run too fast in basketball, you trip over your own feet. When you are young and bright and energetic, you are excited about being successful. Sometimes you have to step back and let the game come to you. Patience is a virtue. Know where the stops are, where the challenges*

Professional Profiles:
Dale Anne Reiss
Global and Americas
Director of Real Estate
Hospitality and Construction
Practices for Ernst & Young

"Clearly, you need many skills to be successful such as technical expertise, presentation skills and especially, sales skills, whatever you are doing, you are really always selling yourself."

Introduction

Ernst & Young (E & Y), one of the Big Four accounting firms, serves clients involved in all aspects of real estate investment, ownership, leasing, construction and in specialty areas such as restaurants, gaming, hospitality and leisure, as well as homebuilding. The firm also produces research for the industry. The global Ernst & Young network boasts 103,000 personnel in more than 140 countries around the world. The corporate headquarters are located in NY.

Education

Reiss received her BA degree in 1968 in Economics and Accounting from the Illinois Institute of Technology and an MBA in Finance and Statistics from University of Chicago in 1970. She is a Certified Public Accountant in Illinois, Florida and New York. *"I believe that formal education is important in a career. I enjoy involvement with schools, and I was an adjunct professor at Illinois Institute of Technology, 1996-1999."*

Career Development:

When Dale Reiss started out in the sixties, real estate was not her chosen profession. Reiss explains, "*When I graduated college at the age of 18, I was too young to sit for the CPA exam. I wanted to get my MBA, but I could not afford school full-time, so I attended the University of Chicago's evening MBA program, and I started work in 1967 as a cost accountant at a major Chicago bank. I was very fortunate, because one of the officers at the bank suggested to me if I really wanted to get ahead, perhaps I should look for employment outside the field of banking, which at the time was not receptive to women. So I took his advice and I went to work as an Assistant Controller for the City Colleges of Chicago from 1967 through 1970. When I left the company, they replaced me with three people, because I had grown up with the organization.*"

Over the years, Reiss continued to excel in several different jobs. From 1970 through 1972, she became Director of Finance for the Department of Public Works in the City of Chicago. She supervised a 50-person department under Mayor Daley when she was only 22 years old. "*In this position, I learned from the ground up about architecture, engineering, and construction of all municipal activities including sewers, high speed rapid transit, filtration plants, and bridges. I was also in charge of all human resources, budgetary and financial activities,*" concludes Reiss.

Her success led her to become a Principal for Arthur Young & Company in Chicago from 1972 to 1980. In this position, Reiss led the financial planning and control consulting practice. She was actively involved in cost accounting, financial systems and strategic planning assignments for a variety of industries including slaughter houses, meat processors, agri-business, public sector and service companies.

From 1980 to 1985, Reiss became the Senior Vice President and Controller for Urban Investment & Development Company in Chicago (A wholly owned subsidiary of Aetna Life & Casualty). She was responsible for the financial and administrative activities of a major national real estate developer. Her job incorporated all development activities including retail, office, mixed use, hotels as well as home building & construction subsidiaries. "*During that time, Urban was building many major developments such as 333 N. Wacker, Water Tower Place and 900 North Michigan in Chicago, and the renovation of the Olympic Hotel in Seattle, and the development of Copley Place in Boston. It was a fabulous time to be with a major development company, and I learned a great deal. It was a great experience, because GAAP (general acceptable accounting principles), earnings and tax, as well as the underlying real estate business, were what made our world go around because of our Aetna parent*" says Reiss.

In 1985, Reiss founded the Chicago office and was the managing partner of Kenneth Leventhal & Company (8th largest accounting firm specializing in real estate). "*When I started at Kenneth Leventhal, I was the only woman managing partner of a Big Eight accounting firm anywhere in the United States, and I learned how to be successful as a woman in both accounting and in real estate.*" Reiss was responsible for overseeing all audit, tax, consulting activities in the Midwest. Her practice grew from a start-up to over 200 people as the most profitable practice in the firm. She served clients including JMB, First National Bank of Chicago, Continental Bank, Homart, and General Growth.

Subsequently, in 1995 Kenneth Leventhal merged into E & Y and in 1999, when Reiss's predecessor retired, she became the Global and Americas Director of Real Estate, Hospitality & Construction practices for Ernst & Young LLP (E & Y), an accomplishment few women could have reached in the industry.

Changes Over The Years

Today in her position as director of E & Y, Reiss is responsible for all real estate, construction, engineering, hospitality, gaming and restaurant practices of the firm, with emphasis on European and Asian integration. Clients she has served personally include Starwood Hotels, Equity Residential, Equity Office, and Tishman Speyer. *"Today, I am in charge of client development, client service, people resources and the growth of audit, tax, mergers and acquisitions, advisory and structuring services. I am involved in numerous IPO's. So I am concerned with all aspects of client service, from obtaining the clients, maintaining client satisfaction, and making sure that the right skills are available in the firm to serve our clients. I spend most of my time traveling to clients, either in the US or globally. I just got back from a three week trip to Dubai and India, because many of our investors are looking at investments in India."*

Personal Side

Over the years, Reiss has worked with many universities: the University of Chicago, Northwestern University, Wharton, Harvard, Columbia University, Baruch, and University of Florida Gulf Coast. She is a Trustee of the Urban Land Institute, Illinois Institute of Technology, Stuart School, Pension Real Estate Association Board of Directors and is a member of the American Institute of Certified Public Accountants, Financial Executives Institute, Institute of Management Consultants, National Association of Real Estate Investment Trusts, The Chicago Network, and the New York Forum. She is a frequent speaker at real estate organizations and has written numerous articles.

Career in Corporate Real Estate

Reiss says, *"I credit my success to my drive in pursuing and taking each opportunity as it was offered along with my willingness to just put one foot in front of another and not give up."*

Career Advice for Real Estate Professionals

Reiss concludes that you must possess several skills to be successful:

1. Know your industry cold. *"You should start with some type of formal education—all types of formal education and degrees are helpful whether it's an MBA, a law degree, a Master's in design, etc, and continue to learn throughout your career. The more you know, the better able you can represent yourself and come up with creative business solution."*
2. Possess general skills. **"***Clearly, you need many skills to be successful such as technical expertise, presentation skills and especially, sales skills, whatever you are doing, you are really always selling yourself."*
3. **Your word is your bond**. *"I am a firm believer in what goes around comes around and you need to develop a reputation over time. I have been in this industry for over 35 years; people know that if they tell me something in private, it will remain confidential. It is a very small world, and you can not burn your bridges."*
4. Grab the opportunities. *"And last, you must be alert to any new opportunity when it presents itself, and then follow the philosophy I believe is set forth in the Nike's phrase, 'just do it.'—that will make all the difference in your ability to more forward in your career."* says Reiss

Professional Profiles: David E. Simon

Chief Executive Officer

Simon Property Group, Inc.

"I believe that the most important factor in your success is for you to have faith and confidence in your abilities"

Introduction

Indianapolis-based real estate development and management company, Simon Property Group, Inc. (SPG), is the largest publicly traded retail Real Estate Investment Trust (REIT) in North America and the country's largest owner, developer and manager of high-quality retail real estate. SPG is a self-administered and self-managed REIT which, through its subsidiary partnership, is engaged primarily in the ownership, development, management, leasing, acquisition and expansion of income-producing retail properties, primarily regional malls, Premium Outlet® centers and community/lifestyle centers. Under David Simon's leadership, SPG has expanded globally, and it currently owns or has an interest in approximately 300 properties in North America and more than 50 properties in Europe and Japan. SPG is a member of the S&P 500 index. SPG's corporate headquarters are in Indianapolis, Indiana.

Career Development

David Simon is the oldest son of Co-chairman Melvin Simon of SPG, who founded SPG with his brother in 1960. Before joining SPG, Mr. Simon was Vice President of Wasserstein Perella & Co., a Wall Street firm specializing in mergers and acquisitions and leveraged buyouts.

David Simon received his Bachelor's of Science degree from Indiana University in 1983, and he earned an MBA from Columbia University's Graduate School of Business in 1985.

He joined the Simon organization in 1990 as Chief Financial Officer and Executive Vice President. Simon says, *"I decided to join the family real estate business after working on Wall Street for several years, because I believed that with my education and work experience in corporate finance and investment banking on Wall Street, I could help the company grow."* Soon after Simon joined the Company, SPG grew rapidly. It went public in 1993, folding most of its properties into Simon Property Group and raising nearly $1 billion, which at the time was the largest real estate stock offering of this type. In 1995, he was named Chief Executive Officer. Following a $3 billion acquisition of DeBartolo Realty Corporation in 1996, the company became Simon DeBartolo Group, the nation's dominant shopping center owner. And in 1998, it became Simon Property Group and is now the No. 1 mall owner in the United States. Simon adds, *"A milestone for me personally at SPG was when in 1998, we bought Corporate Property Investors which at the time was one of the largest real estate M & A transactions – that really created the size and scale in the retail real estate business that beforehand didn't exist. I believe that two other milestones for me personally were when SPG completed four other M & A deals, and when SPG got into the S & P 500 and was recognized as an investment grade company."*

The company has a total market capitalization of approximately $39 billion dollars. SPG owns 78 regional malls located in the 25 largest U.S. metros. The Company's portfolio contains some of the country's most productive and recognizable properties, including: Copley Place, Boston, MA; Dadeland Mall, Miami, FL; The Fashion Centre, Pentagon City, Arlington, VA; The Fashion Valley Mall, San Diego, CA; The Florida Mall, Orlando, FL; The Forum Shops at Caesars, Las Vegas, NV; and The Galleria, Houston, TX .

Changes Over The Years

Under David Simon's leadership, SPG has expanded its operations and become the largest retail REIT in North America. A few projects that SPG is involved with: Clay Terrace in Carmel (Indianapolis), Indiana—a 570,000 square foot upscale lifestyle center (opened 10/04); Arkadia in Warsaw, Poland—a 1.1 million square foot shopping center; St. Johns Town Center in Jacksonville, Florida—a 1.5 million square foot open-air project developed by Simon and Ben Carter Properties (opened 3/05); and Wolf Ranch in Georgetown (Austin), Texas—a 670,000 square foot community center to open in the fall of 2005.

Simon Brand Ventures (SBV), Simon's business-to-consumer arm, has pioneered the transformation of shopping malls into a medium where consumer brands can build one-on-one relationships with shoppers who make approximately 2.2 billion visits to Simon Malls each year. SBV has engaged in a number of consumer business initiatives, including the Simon Giftcard™, launch of Simon platform programs such as Simon Kidgits Club™, Simon Super Chefs Live!™ , Simon DTour Live™.

Simon Business Network (SBN) is the business-to-business division of Simon Property Group. SBN consists of operational programs designed to provide aggregated business solutions for Simon, its retailers and other developers as well as a selection of more than 100 preferred vendors that supply those solutions. Examples of these vendors include KONE, Inc. for vertical transportation needs; Sylvania for lighting.

Simon Global Limited, headquartered in London, is the entity created by SPG through which to pursue its international initiatives. Simon's initial expansion abroad occurred in 1998 with its investment in Groupe B.E.G., a Paris-based developer, owner and manager of retail properties in Europe. In 2003, SPG created a joint venture with The Rinascente Group, an Italian retailer and real estate developer. Gallerie Commerciali Italia S.p.A. was formed to own, manage and develop shopping centers in Italy.

Personal Side

Born in 1961, Simon is a native of Indianapolis, Indiana. Simon spends a great deal of his free time serving in leadership roles in organizations and universities. Mr. Simon is chairman of the National Association of Real Estate Investment Trusts (NAREIT) board of governors and is a former trustee of the International Council of Shopping Centers (ICSC). He has been the recipient of numerous industry honors; in 2000, Mr. Simon was inducted into the Indiana University Kelley School of Business Academy of Alumni Fellows for his support with Indiana University.

His Future Business Plans

Simon describes his goals for SPG: *"We have two main goals for the Company: First, we want to do more international business deals and become a global real estate company. And, secondly, we plan to continue to develop new forms of retail real estate."*

Career in Corporate Real Estate

Simon credits his success as CEO of SPG to several factors: *"I believe that my university education in business and finance combined with my practical experience has helped me succeed. I was able to put the building blocks together to secure my job on Wall Street, which led me to understand corporate finance. This experience enabled me to help take our family business public and ultimately do a number of mergers and acquisitions that allowed us to get to the leadership position that we are in today. Also, I have always had a solid work ethic. I believe as a leader that I am driven, aggressive and hardworking, but more importantly, I try to lead by example."*

Impact of the Internet

Simon believes that technology is changing the retail business: *"I think that technology will continue to help us create efficiency in our business, but we also have to be conscious of how our consumers view and use technology. Often, it is very important for the consumer to have the social experience of shopping at the mall. However, the Internet has had an impact on retailing and it will continue to do so. So, we need to keep an eye on how the consumer wishes to use technology to aid them in shopping. Generally, technology helps us have new opportunities in our business for growth."*

Career Advice for Real Estate Professionals

For a candidate who wants to enter the commercial real estate field, Simon suggests that you should:

1. Have a financial background. *"Since real estate and finance are very closely related, I would suggest that even though you may love bricks and mortar or the development part of the business, you need to also be very skilled in the finance part of the real estate business. Therefore, it is essential for you to understand how the capital markets are part of the equation."*

2. Combine a formal education with practice. *"Without question, a university education will be an aid to you in the business. In addition, I believe that you must also learn through practice."*

3. Be confident. *"I believe that the most important factor in your success is for you to have faith and confidence in your abilities. My situation is a great example of that since I had a lot of opportunities that other students do not have initially, but I had confidence in myself and my abilities to take the Company to the next level. So most importantly, you must believe strongly in yourself and your abilities, and it will lead you forward."*

Professional Profiles:
Nancy Suvarnamani
President
Specialty Group Realty
d/b/a Century 21 S.G.R., Inc.
ABR, CIPS, CRB, RECS

"You must separate yourself from the crowd. People must perceive your value. If they do, you can prosper through your referral network."

Introduction

Soon after moving to America from Thailand, Nancy Suvarnamani founded Specialty Group Realty, Inc. in 1989 with five agents and joined the Century 21 franchise system later in the year. The company is now composed of three offices with over one-hundred agents. The company's sales figures since 1994 have been in the very top echelon of Century 21 companies worldwide. The firm has expanded beyond the marketing and sale of properties into investment partnerships that supply much of the capital for their developments. Over 1/3 of the business currently is with commercial properties. Through Suvarnamani's international relationships, her firm does business with clients in Thailand as well as other parts of the world.

Education

After graduating with a BA from Chiengmai University in Thailand in 1972 with a major in finance, Suvarnamani came to the United States in 1974 to pursue her graduate studies. She says, *"I came to the US because I had earned a scholarship to take a Master of Science Degree. I wanted to get an education to teach information technology and science in a university. I dreamed of becoming a professor even though I knew that professors did not make a great deal of money. At the time, I was working for Beatrice Foods."* She earned a MA from Northeastern Illinois University in 1976 and a MS from Northern Illinois University in 1978. In addition, she has received many real estate certifications including: Certified International Property Specialist designation (CIPS), NAR's Council of Real Estate Brokerage Managers (CRB), Accredited Buyer Representative (ABR) and Real Estate CyberSpace Specialist (RECS).

Career Development

Prior to entering real estate, Suvarnamani was a branch manager at the Bangkok Bank in Thailand from 1972 – 1974. *"I then came to the United States and found employment with the Beatrice Foods Company in their Research and Development Department from 1974-1981. I next worked in the Research and Development Department of the Borg Warner Corporation for three years. My informational research career ended after a one year stint with the Gas Research Institute. At this time, I unequivocally knew that I wanted more control over my destiny than that offered by a rigidly stratified research career. While working at the Gas Research Institute, I attained my real estate license and started working part time at Century 21 Illinois Home. Almost immediately, I knew that I had finally discovered my niche in the world of work. I was enrolled in the Master's program, and I started working part time in real estate. I learned that in the real estate field there are unlimited possibilities to make money. The business is like going fishing in the ocean; you can fish all night in the ocean, because there are unlimited fish to catch. I also learned that regardless of your culture, sex, age or language, if you work hard the possibilities to make money and do a great service for people are unlimited. So I began working in real estate business full time. After 14 years of doing what I was trained to do – I finally discovered what I wanted to do. Within a year, I got my broker's license and went to work full time first as the sales manager of Casablanca Realty then as a sales manager for a branch of Century 21 Full Service. Within 18 months of joining Century 21 Full Service, I opened my own firm."*

Changes Over The Years

Once ensconced in the Century 21 system, Suvarnamani had to learn quickly how to run a business, so she attended an Operation Orbit Program in their International Management Academy. In one years time, the program taught new brokers/owners and managers from around the world every facet of the real estate experience they would encounter. Dr. Dick McKenna guided participants through the theoretical and practical aspects of establishing a viable business. "*To this day I attribute much of my success to Professor McKenna who helped me to understand how to communicate with the many people that would affiliate with my firm. Operation Orbit probably saved me years of groping blindly for solutions that I readily employed upon exposure to them in my business.*"

Personal Side

Suvarnamani grew up in Bangkok in a rather privileged environment. Her father is a retired Major General, and her mother a registered nurse. Suvarnamani travels a great deal both for personal and professional reasons. "*I devote much of my time today to the growth and strengthening of the Chicago Association of Realtors (CAR), the third largest realtor association in the United States. I will assume the Presidency of CAR in September 2005,* I *have represented CAR in the international community many times including leading a delegation to Bangkok, Thailand, Madrid, Athens, Latvia, Houston, New York, and Washington D.C."*

Future Plans

Suvarnamani has delegated much of the day-to-day operations of the firm to colleagues who have been with her for years. Her company is continually growing business of commercial properties as well as sales of residential. The firm has expanded beyond the marketing of properties into investment rise in the South Loop and a 40-unit mid-rise in the West Loop. *"We have several additional projects on-line for which we will supply all or part of the equity capital consisting of 240 units spread over 4 sites. My offices have consistently received the Century 21 Quality Service Award, signifying that over 95% of clients have rated their experience with Century 21 S.G.R. as highly positive*," adds Suvarnamani. In 2002, 2003, 2004, and 2005 the company received the prestigious President's Award, which signifies both an extraordinary level of production and an extremely high degree of custom satisfaction

Career Advice for Real Estate Professionals

1. Education. *"The opportunities to make money for anyone who wants to work hard and learn are endless today in America. I would love other women and minorities to realize that there are scholarships available in the United States to take college programs. Education is important for everyone today in business. You must know more about your business arena than anyone else—this takes a commitment to education that continues throughout your career."*

2. Develop a Niche. *"You cannot be all things to all people. You must become an expert on a neighborhoods or a certain product type within a city. You should know one product better than anyone else – whether that product be a type of housing, a community, or something else. You must separate yourself from the crowd. People must perceive your value. If they do, you can prosper through your referral network."*

3. Develop Business Partnerships. *"If you want to establish a business, you must enter into a business partnership. Incumbent upon all new business owners is the need to learn the business intimately, to develop a niche, and to service*

this niche once established. This will take time and capital. If you don't have the capital needed to sustain your business, wait until you do. The number 1 reason most businesses fail is because they lack the capital to sustain the learning and growth stages all business must pass through."

4. Join Organizations. "*You should join professional associations. You will build business and personal relationships and help support your field.*"

Profesional Profiles:
Ruth Theobald
CPM®, HCCP
President and owner
TheoPro Compliance
& Consulting, Inc.

"I have learned that your instincts will tell you what is right for you, but you have to make a decision on how to organize to proceed. You should organize your time, space and life so that you can go after a career that is right for you."

Introduction:

Ruth L. Theobald is a nationally recognized property manager, trainer and consultant in affordable housing properties. Theobald is a very successful business woman and well-known real estate writer who has her own column called "Dr. Ruth" in *Affordable Housing Magazine*. Her company, TheoPro, produces seminars and workshops around the country specializing in the management of tax credit housing. Theobald has over 23 years of experience in property management in the Midwest, particularly in Wisconsin. Theobald has 18 years of day-to-day management and marketing of real estate properties and more than 17 years experience designing and conducting training seminars and consulting with companies on issues related to subsidized housing properties.

Education:

Theobald is a licensed real-estate broker and a certified property manager (CPM). She is a member of the Institute of Real Estate Management (IREM), and she was the 1996 president of the Milwaukee chapter. Since 1994, she has been a member of the IREM 101 course faculty and received its "Academy of Excellence" award for teaching in 1995. She has also been a part-time faculty member at Waukesha County Technical College. She is a training partner for the NAHB's HCCP Certification course and exam. As a member of the NAHB Housing Credit Group committee responsible for creating the Housing Credit Certified Partner (HCCP) exam, she is an approved trainer for this prestigious certification.

Career Development:

In 1981, Theobald began working in property management. In 1987, she joined Affiliated Capital Corporation (ACC), a full-service property management company based in Wisconsin. Soon after, she became the vice president and director of property management of ACC. In this position, Theobald provided training, marketing, management, and consulting on many forms of government-subsidized housing throughout the United States. Theobald says, "*I started working in the field of property management in 1981. And in 1987, I started working for Affiliated Capital. I worked very closely with the Milwaukee developer. For 14 years, I helped him on the development side and also managed his multi-family real estate division. We had also developed a tax credit consulting business together, and I was really the nucleus of this training business. Over the years, I had grown personally and financially in every way, and. I kept asking him, 'Can I please be a partner?' And he'd say, 'No. I don't want any partners.' Finally, I had built enough of a client base that I got strong enough to ask him if I became an independent consultant and could build a business, would he be my partner? And so, we partnered in 1998, and he gave me a piece of ownership in the software, and I gave him a piece of ownership in the consulting business. As I continued to focus on my career, I realized that I needed to be completely on my own. And in May of 2001, we un-partnered and I changed the company name from Affiliated Compliance and Consulting to TheoPro Consulting.*"

Changes Over The Years:

Since she opened her own company, TheoPRO, Theobald has become even more successful. *"Complete ownership of my business gives me a sense of being a whole person as well as the tremendous financial benefits. It may work for other people to be dependent on somebody else financially, but it never worked for me."* She is considered to be one of the top trainer/consultants in affordable housing in the United States. Theobald's focus is the successful development and compliance management of tax credit housing. The firm's clients include investors and syndicators, developers, management agents of tax credit housing around the country. Its emphasis is on the compliance management of tax credit housing. TheoPRO produces seminars and workshops around the country for industry professionals. Currently the only *public* provider of the Housing Credit Certified Professional (HCCP) review and exam, TheoPRO actively promotes and endorses this prestigious certification. TheoPRO also provides a variety of services including approval, review and audit services, and special projects. TheoPRO team applies its knowledge and years of experience to the careful and conservative protection of tax credit housing. The corporate office is located near Milwaukee, Wisconsin.

Personal Side:

Theobald has always enjoyed writing for business and pleasure. She enjoys contributing to her famous monthly 'Dr. Ruth' in *Affordable Housing Magazine*, and Theobald has also written for the *Journal of Property Management*. She has also formed an educational company called *Lifemark Institute for Greatness* that publishes her own books and journals. *"I have always loved to write. A few years ago, I set aside time to write down my thoughts on the subject in my journal every morning for 30 minutes. And through writing, I was finally able to look at my financial goals and desire to make a tremendous amount of money, and it has helped me open two companies and reach a tremendous level of personal and financial success for a woman in business today, especially in real estate."* She often lectures across the country on real estate and career success. Theobald has been a featured speaker at state and national conferences, including Multi-Housing World conferences and IREM. She also had been featured in a national video, "Compliance: Managing Tax Credits," produced by the Consortium for Housing Assistance Managers in Washington.

Her Future Business Plans

In today's complex world, property management for affordable housing properties has become a sophisticated business. TheoPRO's extensive background in government-assisted housing property management serves as a base from which these services are provided. *"The interplay between management and compliance issues are particularly sensitive in Section 42 housing, and I continue to build my company with additional staff and services in affordable housing as well as develop my new business ventures with books and journals,"* adds Theobald.

Impact of Technology:

New technologies have enabled Theobald to increase her business dramatically. In the last 17 years, Theobald became involved in the design, training and sale of the new software technology called ACCuCERT to help with the accounting procedures of affordable housing projects. "*With all the regulations and paper work involved to meet regulations, we are able to provide superior service to our clients through emails and our terrific software program."*

Career Advice for Real Estate Professionals

Theobald suggests that to be successful in corporate real estate as business owner, you have to get a point where you can focus on the possibilities.

1. Take time to organize. "*I have learned that your instincts will tell you what is right for you, but you have to make a decision on how to organize to proceed. You should organize your time, space and life so that you can go after a career that is right for you.*"

2. Consider Ownership. *Especially if you are a woman, you should consider, as I did, the many financial and professional benefits of owning your own company"* says Theobald.

Professional Profiles: Samuel (Sam) Zell

Chairman
Equity Group Investments

"Trust yourself and choose to act with a strong conviction."

Introduction

Samuel Zell, founder of the modern Real Estate Investment Trust (REIT) industry and economic visionary, and has often been referred to as one of the most influential business leaders and entrepreneurs in the world. He is well known for his perceptive and shrewd economic foresight.

Education

Mr. Zell is a graduate of the University of Michigan and the University of Michigan Law School.

Career History

Sam Zell began his career in real estate while an undergraduate at the University of Michigan by managing apartment buildings throughout Southeast Michigan. He continued his interests in real estate with the founding of Equity Financial and Management Co., now Equity Group Investments, L.L.C., an entrepreneurial private investment firm based in Chicago where he is Chairman of the Board.

With his late partner, Robert Lurie, Mr. Zell sought out and capitalized on numerous real estate opportunities in the 1970s and 1980s, building a substantial private portfolio of residential, office, manufactured home and retail assets. In the

1990s, he brought this portfolio to the public markets when he founded three of the nation's largest self-administered and self-managed REITs in their respective asset classes: Equity Residential (NYSE: EQR), Equity Office Properties Trust (NYSE: EOP), and Equity Lifestyle Properties (formerly Manufactured Home Communities, Inc.) (NYSE:ELS). Mr. Zell remains Chairman of these publicly-traded companies.

Mr. Zell also maintains substantial interests in and serves as Chairman of the Board of Anixter International (NYSE: AXE), a value-added provider of integrated networking and cabling solutions that support business information and network infrastructure requirements; Capital Trust (NYSE: CT), a specialized real estate finance company; and Rewards Network Inc. (AMEX: IRN), a leading provider of dining rewards programs.

Personal Information

A Chicago native, Mr. Zell is an avid skier, racquetball player and enjoys riding motorcycles. He is a frequent contributor to various publications and is often heard as a keynote speaker throughout the United States and Europe. Mr. Zell recently completed a two-year term as Chairman of the National Association of Real Estate Investment Trusts (NAREIT). He serves on the JPMorgan National Advisory Board, the EuroHYPO International Advisory Board, the President's Advisory Board at the University of Michigan, and the Visitor's Committee at the University of Michigan Law School. He established the Zell/Lurie Entrepreneurial Center at the University of Michigan Business School. Mr. Zell's continual assistance to the University of Michigan's MBA program has also enhanced the Business School's Polish Studies Program. He was appointed a DeRoy Visiting Professor in Honors at the College of Literature, Science and the Arts at the University of Michigan. He is a long standing supporter of the University of Pennsylvania Wharton Real Estate Center and has endowed the Samuel Zell/Robert Lurie Real Estate Center at Wharton. Mr. Zell has also endowed the Northwestern University Center for Risk Management.

Visionary Thinking

For more than 40 years, Sam Zell has established an outstanding reputation as an opportunistic investor, financier, builder and operator of industry-leading companies. He has succeeded in ways others thought impossible. As the nation's largest private landlord, Mr. Zell has challenged the notion that all real estate is local, driving Equity Office to become the country's only true national office real estate owner and operator and Equity Residential to become the largest publicly-traded owner, operator and developer of multifamily housing in the United States. Both companies are also listed in the S&P 500 and have been recognized by Fortune magazine as being among the "Most Admired Companies in America." Equity Lifestyle Properties owns and operates the highest quality portfolio of resort communities in the United States.

His real estate vision expands beyond U.S. borders. Equity International Properties is a privately-held company that invests in real estate businesses outside of the United States. The company strategically co-invests with world-class local partners in existing and newly-formed foreign real estate companies that have meaningful growth potential. Ever the contrarian, Mr. Zell and Equity International focus on geographic regions—such as Latin America, Central and Eastern Europe, India and China—that are characterized by strong economic growth yet also experience limited capital market efficiency and limited competition. Equity International has been at the vanguard of institutionalizing developing markets such as Mexico. There, it is one of the most active real estate investors with five portfolio companies, including Homex, a leading publicly-held homebuilder (NYSE:HXM).

Mr. Zell is well-known for possessing many outstanding leadership abilities. He is ambitious, self-confident, motivated, focused, self-disciplined, a great salesman and an eternal optimist, making him the consummate entrepreneur. When asked to explain how his leadership style as an entrepreneur has enabled him to become one of the world's most successful real estate businessmen, Mr. Zell says, *"I have been very fortunate in that I have developed an enormous self-confidence and that self-confidence has allowed me to be different and survive. And, therefore, I have been successful as a contrarian in identifying where I think the opportunities are, and then implementing the strategies accordingly."*

Staying Ahead of the Curve

Although Mr. Zell believes that new technologies improve business efficiency, he says that technology is only one aspect that illustrates how business is becoming more complex. Mr. Zell explains, *"The skills required to succeed in business are constantly changing. The real estate business is becoming more and more sophisticated. As our knowledge level increases, we have a greater ability to expand into and create markets throughout the world. And with increased knowledge, we can better quantify and assess the risks, identify new opportunities, and ultimately be more successful."*

Future Opportunities

When asked about his future, Mr. Zell says, *"I am always looking for the next opportunity. I like to test my limits and have a high level of curiosity. Taking risks is an important part of what I do. I am very comfortable with risks, and learn from each adventure. Today, I certainly do things a little differently than I did a few years ago. And I suspect the real challenge—'the testing of my limits'—will be whether I can continue to change efficiently and continue to see and take advantage of opportunities."*

Career Advice for Real Estate Professionals

Zell offers some advice for students interested in pursuing a career in real estate:

1. Get real world experience: *"A university education is wonderful; it teaches you analytical and thinking skills. But you also need to understand how businesses, and how real estate in particular, functions. If I were starting out today, I would seek an interim position that would give me a real grounding in the elements of the business. The best thing to do is pick a bank or an insurance company, or pick someplace where you can really get a ground floor education."*

2. Think like an entrepreneur: *"If you think like an entrepreneur, the scope of career opportunities to become world class leaders for new venture creation is broad. An entrepreneurial mindset is also a valuable asset for anyone seeking to pursue entrepreneurship within the bounds of a corporate structure."*

3. Salesmanship is key: *"You can't be successful if you are not a great salesman. You have to be able to take your ideas and sell them to others. A great salesman is not like the image that Willie Loman portrayed in the 'Death of a Salesman,' but instead, one who knows how to take his/her ideas and sell them to get support. You must see the importance of selling and being able to clearly communicate your business ideas."*

4. Calibrate your risks, but be action oriented: *"You should calibrate the risks to succeed, but you must be a risk-taker and you cannot be afraid to act. Trust yourself and choose to act with a strong conviction."*

5. Test your limits: In typical Zell style, he ends with a quote by Daniel Burnham, a famous Chicago architect, which summed up his views on life: *"Make no little plans. They have no magic to stir men's blood. And probably they will not be realized."* Mr. Zell concludes, *"I strongly believe in Burnham's ideas that you should make big plans. Find where your talents are and aim high -- always test your limits."*

Steve Felix
Senior Vice President
of Institutional
Real Estate Inc. (IREI)

What advice would you give to a student who is focused on the real estate industry?

Edited from a presentation on February 21st 2005 to The Kellogg School Real Estate Club based on his own views and those of his friends.

1. Learn the numbers behind the deals. Learn ARGUS or similar software as well as Excel.
2. Learn to play golf.
3. Take any internship, even if you must work for free.
4. Learn financial analysis.
5. Work as an appraiser or at least learn what drives value.
6. Respect the importance of the Human Resource and Organizational Behavior courses and pay attention to them. If you advance into senior management and/or principal positions someday HR and OB issues will dominate your lives.
7. Go for the person vs. the company. That is, choose good and talented colleagues.
8. Learn how to value the asset, develop judgment and build relationships.
9. Learn the leasing part of the business. Be an operator in

property management, leasing, or construction management. Even if you know you want to end up in finance or development, the only way the numbers mean anything is if you actually know what's involved in executing your assumptions. Every great Real Estate entrepreneur I ever met started in an operations part of the business.

10. Be willing to learn from the ground up. Lose the attitude.

11. The business used to be "location, location, location". Now it's "manager, manager, manager". The most important thing you can do is to properly examine the character of any firm you are interested in joining. All the other stuff is just stuff!

12. Add value and do more than you are asked. Be effective; don't just put in hours.

13. If you really just have to get a tattoo make sure it's in a place where it doesn't show in a job interview.

14. Get to know all clients...understand their needs...respond with solutions.

15. Learn the art and science of negotiating.

16. Go somewhere where you can participate in or, at a minimum, observe the deal making process.

17. Develop good writing and presentation skills.

18. Don't forget to take time off before life becomes a lot more complicated.

19. Be honest with yourself about what you enjoy doing but expect to first pay your dues. You don't know as much as you think you do.

20. People that are happy at what they are doing perform much better than those that are unhappy.

21. Be very passionate about the industry, not just drawn to it because it's currently popular and a "hot industry". The best real estate professionals have it their blood and they know by how they are drawn to real estate entrepreneurs, their stories and deals. The excitement and passion will be obvious and the internships and jobs will materialize as a result.

22. Gain experience leasing properties and understanding

tenant needs. Also, try to participate in running the numbers and the financing of properties.

23. Evaluate your own personal strengths and the type of environment you thrive in and then look to focus in that arena. This could entail personality profile testing or just a candid assessment of what you love and want.

24. Join local trade-groups and networking clubs.

25. Never underestimate the power of relationships. People you fire may end up your clients, companies you leave may end up with the biggest RFP in the city, and someone opposite you in a deal may end up a key decision-maker whose respect you need.

26. Never do or say anything you don't want to see as a headline in the paper the next day.

27. There are no secrets that are forever kept. The only difference is how long they take to become known.

27. Tenants should never see you as their "friend". The best way to be known is "firm, but fair".

28. If a document has your signature on it, know what every single thing on that piece of paper means. If a client feels you're unprepared on one item they will question everything you do. Always over-prepare.

29. If you get into a tough situation, deal with it head on. Raise your hand early, before "concerns" become "problems". Hiding something you're worried about always makes it worse.

30. Take the personal out of your reactions. Deals, people, co-workers, employees, and tenants will inevitably "get to you". Remember its business, and problems will always arise. People will judge your abilities not on how well you "maintain", but how well you "maintain under pressure".

31. Find a mentor.

32. Have an open mind, be flexible and be enthusiastic. With regard to open-mindedness, the student should recognize that there are many ways to participate in the real estate business. It matters less where you start than what you make of it.

33. Consider contacting alumni for network assistance.

34. Look at small as well as large firms.
35. Love what you do, whatever it is.
36. Treat all people with respect.
37. Have patience with people whose speaking of English is not as good as yours.
38. Be impeccable with your word. [1]
39. Don't take anything personally.
40. Don't make assumptions.
41. Always do your best.
42. Be curious.
43. Remember that first impressions last.
44. Trust your hunches. [2]
45. Give people a great deal of authority.
46. Treat people with real dignity and listen. Ask them how things could be done better.
47. Money is secondary.
48. Great leaders make themselves dispensable by creating organizations that function without them.
49. Choose wisely. [3]
50. The school you come from matters less than who you are. Attitude matters more than anything else. Be self-confident but honest. An interesting read is the book "Nuts" which describes Southwest's corporate culture.

---

1 Numbers 4, 5, 6 from The Four Agreements by Don Miguel Ruiz

2 Numbers 10-13 from comments on business by John Cleese (Yes, the Monty Python one)

3 From Indiana Jones: The Last Crusade

Professional Profiles
compiled by:
Dr. Margot B. Weinstein

Dr. Margot B. Weinstein is a successful commercial real estate practitioner, consultant, speaker, educator and writer in the fields of real estate and human resource development with over 30 years experience. Dr. Weinstein is President and CEO of MW Leadership Consultants LLC and Vice President of Kingston Group Inc., a commercial real estate company based in Illinois.

Dr. Weinstein has strong research interests in many areas of commercial real estate education including designing leadership strategies from her research to add new insights to real estate education. Dr. Weinstein has interviewed over 100 real estate leaders and is published in more than 55 publications. She has lectured at several universities, organizations and professional associations.

In 1998, Dr. Weinstein received her doctorate from Northern Illinois University and was initiated into Kappa Delta Pi International Honor Society. Her dissertation on leaders in real estate was nominated for the dissertation of the year. She is also an award winning developer recognized for a Good Neighbor's Award from the prestigious Chicago Association of REALTORS®. She earned two masters' degrees from National-Louis University in Illinois: one in psychology and one in adult education. Dr. Weinstein did her post-doctoral research in Finland and Russia in 2000 in human resource development, adult education and real estate. She became a Certified International Property Specialist (CIPS) Designate in 2002. She serves on several boards, and she is an active member of many organizations.

Part 5

Glossary

General Glossary of Key Real Estate Terms

Abstract (Of Title): A summary of the public records relating to the title to a particular piece of land. An attorney or title insurance company reviews an abstract of title to determine whether there are any title defects which must be cleared before a buyer can purchase clear, marketable, and insurable title.

Acceleration Clause: Condition in a mortgage that may require the balance of the loan to become due immediately, if regular mortgage payments are not made or for breach of other conditions of the mortgage.

ADA: Americans with Disabilities Act, passed by the Federal government of the USA on July 26, 1990 to establish a clear and comprehensive prohibition of discrimination on the basis of disability. See www.usdoj.gov/crt/ada/adahom1.htm

Agent: An authorized person who manages or transacts business for another called the principal.

Agreement of Sale: Known by various names, such as contract of purchase, purchase agreement, or sales agreement according to location or jurisdiction. A contract in which a seller agrees to sell and a buyer agrees to buy, under certain specific terms and conditions spelled out in writing and signed by both parties.

Amortize: To pay a debt in periodic amounts until the total amount, including any interest, is paid. To "amortize" is also to write off against taxable income something over time such as mortgage points.

Appraisal: A qualified party's opinion of the value of a property; an expert judgment or estimate of the quality or value of real estate as of a given date.

Appreciation: Expressed as a percentage, the return generated from either inflation or real price change. Investors prefer real price increases, those beyond the rate of inflation, since these are generated by demand growing relative to supply and real estate tends to move with inflation in the long run anyway simply as a durable asset.

ARM (Adjustable Rate Mortgage): A financing technique in which the lender can raise or lower the mortgage interest rate according to a set index, such as Treasury bills.

Assessment: An official valuation of property for tax purposes. Also payments made by condominium or cooperative owners for their share of building maintenance expenses.

Asset Manager: Acquire and dispose of property, decide when to increase investment in a property to generate additional income, may select and supervise property manager.

BOMA Standard: The dominant standard for building measurements provided by BOMA, "Building Owners and Managers Association". See www.boma.org.

Broker: An independent business person who sets real estate office policies, hires employees, determines their compensation, and supervises their activities in the role of a real estate intermediary or agent.

Brownfield: A site perceived to be or actually contaminated by pollutants from prior uses or nearby site underground, surface runoff and airborne contamination. Requires phase 1 inspection to assess actual condition, phase 2 study to determine remediation steps required for clean up and Phase 3 implementation of actual cleanup. The EPA provides a certification after clean up has reached acceptable standards. There are hundreds of brownfield sites in most major cities. See http://www.epa.gov/brownfields/

Building Codes: A set of standards enforced by the local government that require certain materials, design, building processes, safety features and inspections as a building is constructed. Intended to protect both those who build the structure as well as those who may live or visit the structure.

Buyer Agent: An agent who represents the buyer in a real estate transaction. A buyer agent may be paid by the buyer, seller, or listing agent at closing, provided all parties consent.

Capital Expenditures: Additional physical improvements, e.g., land, buildings, building additions, site improvements, machinery, equipment; lighting, roofing, HVAC systems, cables, as distinguished from cash outflows for items that are normally considered part of the current property operations.

CBD: Central Business District or downtown, except in Charlotte, NC where downtown is "uptown".

CERCLA: Comprehensive Environmental Response, Compensation, and Liability Act, also known as the "Superfund" act, gives EPA the authority to respond directly to releases or threatened releases of hazardous substances that may endanger human health or the environment. See http://es.epa.gov/oeca/osre/superfund.html

Certificate of Title: A certificate issued by a title company or a written opinion rendered by an attorney that the seller has good marketable and insurable title to the property which he is offering for sale. A certificate of title offers no protection against any hidden defects in the title that an examination of the records could not reveal. The issuer of a certificate of title is liable only for damages due to negligence. The protection offered a homeowner under a certificate of title is not as great as that offered in a title insurance policy.

Closing Costs: The numerous expenses which buyers and sellers normally incur to complete a transaction in the transfer of ownership of real estate. These costs are in addition to price of the property and are items prepaid at the closing day.

CMA (Competitive Market Analysis): A method of determining the value of a property by comparing the prices paid for similar properties.

CMBS: Collateralized Mortgage Backed Securities, large pools of commercial mortgages that have been rated by credit agencies and sold in tranches (slices of varying risk and terms).

Code of Ethics: A written standard of ethical conduct embraced by the affected trade association to describe appropriate business conduct under a variety of circumstances. The emphasis in most codes of ethics is on truthful representation, avoidance of conflicts of interest, respect for colleagues, and open disclosure of areas of competency and experience.

Commission: Compensation paid to a real estate agent (usually by the seller) for services rendered in connection with the sale, exchange, or lease of property.

Condemnation: The taking of private property for public use by a government unit, against the will of the owner, but with payment of just compensation under the government's power of eminent domain. Condemnation may also be based on a determination by a governmental agency that a particular building is unsafe or unfit for use.

Condominium (Condo): Individual ownership of a portion of a building, with common areas shared by all owners. Maintenance fees called "assessments" are paid to the condominium association to maintain, repair, or improve the property.

Contract: Legal agreement between a buyer and seller or tenant and landlord that is in writing and includes all the elements necessary for a legally binding contract; consideration, signed authority, descriptions, closing date, contingencies, and the process to remove contingencies at a minimum.

Contractor: In the construction industry, a contractor is one who contracts to erect buildings or portions of them. There are also contractors for each phase of construction: heating, electrical, plumbing, air conditioning, and others.

Corporate Facilities Manager: Responsible for site selection, acquisition, construction, lease negotiation, furniture, operations, accounting, and labor management for industrial and service corporations.

Cost Approach to Value: The current cost to construct a reproduction of, or replacement for, the existing structure less an estimate for accrued depreciation, plus the prepared site cost.

Deed: A formal written instrument by which title to real property is transferred from one owner to another. The deed should contain an accurate description of the property being conveyed, should be signed and witnessed according to the laws of the State where the property is located, and should be delivered to the purchaser at closing day. There are two parties to a deed: the grantor and the grantee

Default: Failure to make mortgage payments as agreed to in a commitment based on the terms and at the designated time set forth in the mortgage or deed of trust. It is the mortgagor's responsibility to remember the due date and send the payment prior to the due date, not after. In the event of default, the mortgage may give the lender the right to accelerate payments, take possession and receive rents, and start foreclosure. Defaults may also come about by the failure to observe other conditions in the mortgage or deed of trust.

Depreciation: Decline in value of a property due to wear and tear, adverse changes in the neighborhood, or any other reason. Also for commercial property depreciation refers to the economic life over which the asset, excluding land, might be written off for the calculation of taxable income. Current economic lives for residential investment property are 27.5 years and 39.0 years for commercial property.

Developer: Responsible for initiating and coordinating all the activities necessary for project development including design, financing, site acquisition, preparation, permitting and lease-up. The developer's ownership role might be anywhere from 0% to 100

Discount Rate: A yield rate used to convert future payments or receipts into present value.

Down Payment: A percentage of the purchase price the buyer pays in cash typically at the closing; the amount of money to be paid by the purchaser to the seller upon the transfer of title. The down payment is the difference between the sales price and mortgage loan also known as initial equity.

Dual Agent: An agent representing both parties in a transaction. In almost every state, dual agency is illegal and unethical without the written consent of both the buyer and the seller.

Earnest Money: The same thing as consideration or a deposit. The money given to the seller or his agent by the potential buyer upon the signing of the agreement of sale to show that he is serious about buying the property and to form a binding contract.

Easement: A right-of-way granted to a person or company authorizing access to or over the owner's land. An electric company obtaining a right-of-way across private property is a common example.

Escrow: Funds paid by one party to another (the escrow agent) to hold until the occurrence of a specified event, after which the funds are released to a designated individual.

Exclusive Listing: A written agreement in which the seller appoints only one agent to market the property for a specific period of time. If the owner sells or leases the property himself, he is not required to pay a commission.

Exclusive Right of Sale Listing: A written agreement between an agent and a property owner stating that the owner will pay a commission to the agent if the property is sold during a specific time period whether or not the agent is responsible for the sale.

Fair Market Value: The price a property will command on the open market, neither buyer or seller acting under duress and with full information. Statistically, fair market value is the most probable selling price with a typical marketing period.

Fannie Mae (Federal National Mortgage Association): Fannie Mae purchases home mortgages, thus serving as a source of funds for mortgage lenders. It is a privately owned corporation whose shares are traded on the New York Stock Exchange, but it is subject to the strict supervision of the secretary of the U.S. Department of Housing and Urban Development (HUD).

Federal Fair Housing Law: Refers to Title VIII of the Civil Rights Act, and stipulates that discrimination based on race, color, sex, familial status, handicap, religion, or national origin is illegal in connection with the sale or rental of most dwellings.

FHA (Federal Housing Administration): A federal agency established to improve housing standards and conditions. The FHA provides mortgage insurance to approved lending institutions.

Foreclosure: A legal term applied to any of the various methods of enforcing payment of the debt secured by a mortgage, or deed of trust, by taking and selling the mortgaged property.

Freddie Mac (Federal Home Loan Mortgage Corporation): Once a federally chartered corporation established to purchase mortgages in the secondary, or resale market it is now a private corporation. It is subject to some oversight by the U.S. Department of Housing and Urban Development (HUD).

General Warranty Deed: A deed which conveys not only all the grantor's interests in and title to the property to the grantee, but also warrants that if the title is defective or has a "cloud" on it (such as mortgage claims, tax liens, title claims, judgments, or mechanic's liens against it) the grantee may hold the grantor liable.

Grantee: That party in the deed who is the buyer or recipient.

Grantor: That party in the deed who is the seller or giver.

Green Design: A term that describes attempts to consider the impact of development including parking lots, building design, operation and building recycling on the environment. Lighting and energy uses more efficient options and people sensitive systems that turn off when no one is around. Windows are reflective and all possible materials are made in such a way as to be recycled.

GSA: General Services Administration; entity that manages approximately 40% of the federal government's office space

Guaranty: A pledge made by one person (the guarantor) to ensure that another person (the obligor) will fulfill an obligation to a third party (the obligee).

Hazard Insurance: Protects against damages caused to property by fire, windstorms, and other common hazards.

Highest and Best Use: The reasonably probable and legal use of vacant land or an improved property which is physically possible, appropriately supported, financially feasible, and that results in the highest value.

HUD (U.S. Department of Housing and Urban Development): A federal department active in a variety of national housing programs including urban renewal and public housing.

HVAC: Heating, Ventilating and Air Conditioning

Improvements: Buildings and additions intended to increase the value of a property.

Income Capitalization Value: The indication of value derived for an income-producing property by converting its anticipated net operating income into property value by direct capitalization of expected income, where value equals the NOI divided by the capitalization rate.

Lien: A charge or claim by one party on the property of another as security for the payment of a debt. Such claims may include obligations not met or satisfied, judgments, unpaid taxes, materials, or labor.

Listing Agent: The agent who represents the seller.

Listing: A written agreement between a property owner and a real estate broker authorizing the broker to find a buyer or tenant.

Marketable Title: A title that is free and clear of objectionable liens, clouds, or other title defects. A title which enables an owner to sell his property freely to others and which others will accept without objection.

Material Defect: Any attribute affecting property value that is not readily observable but which might be known by the seller of such property must be disclosed to residential buyers under most state laws using state mandated disclosure forms.

MLS (Multiple Listing Service): A means by which agents list properties offered for sale by other agents, often available through the internet to the public.

Mortgage Commitment: A written notice from the bank or other lending institution saying it will advance mortgage funds in a specified amount to enable a buyer to purchase a property.

Mortgage Note: A written agreement to repay a loan. The agreement is secured by a mortgage, serving as proof of indebtedness, and states the manner in which it shall be paid.

Mortgage: A legal document pledging property as security for the payment of a loan and a lien or claim against real property given by the buyer to the lender as security for money borrowed.

Mortgagee: The lender in a mortgage agreement.

Mortgagor: The borrower in a mortgage agreement.

NAIOP: National Association of Industrial and Office Properties. See www.naiop.org

Net Sales Proceeds: Proceeds from the sale of an asset or part of an asset less brokerage commissions, closing costs, legal and marketing expenses.

Offer: A proposal to purchase property at a specified price and terms.

Origination Fee: A lender's charge for establishing and processing a new mortgage loan. It is generally computed as a percentage of the loan and may be tax deductible.

Owner of Record: The person or entity named in the public record as the owner of a property or mortgage.

Partnership: An association of two or more persons or entities for the purpose of carrying out an investment or business for profit and for sharing of both profits and losses.

Phase 1, 2, 3 Inspections and Studies: Phase 1 is a historical review and inspection of a site to determine if there are likely any environmental concerns. A phase 2 study involves soil borings, tests for toxic presences and estimates the extent of cleanup necessary. Phase 3 is the actual clean up of a site.

Plat: A map or chart of a lot, subdivision or community drawn by a surveyor showing boundary lines, buildings, improvements on the land, and easements.

Points: A one-time charge paid to the lender for issuing a loan. Each point equals one percent of the loan amount and is used to obtain revenue in addition to the interest rate. Sometimes called "discount points." For example, if a loan is for $250,000, one point is $2,500. Points are charged by a lender to raise the yield on the loan at closing.

Prepayment: Payment of mortgage loan, or part of it before the due date. Mortgage agreements often restrict the right of prepayment either by limiting the amount that can be prepaid in any one year or charging a penalty for prepayment. Some loans are "locked out" preventing early pre-payment.

Property Manager: Property managers are responsible for the care and upkeep of the premises and often coordinate leasing activities either directly or through the designated leasing agent.

Property Tax: As applied to real estate, an enforced charge imposed on persons, property or income, to be used to support the State. The governing body in turn utilizes the funds to support public services such as schools.

Punch list: Items yet to be completed during new construction based on an inspection by the buyer or tenant.

Purchase Price: The total cost of an investment including all amounts paid to the seller excluding any adjustments at closing.

Qualified Buyer: A buyer who has demonstrated the financial ability to afford the asking price of a property.

Quitclaim Deed: A deed which transfers whatever interest the maker of the deed may have in the particular parcel of land. A quitclaim deed is often given to clear the title when the grantor's interest in a property is questionable. By accepting such a deed the buyer assumes all the risks. Such a deed makes no warranties as to the title, but simply transfers to the buyer whatever interest the grantor has. (See deed.)

REALTOR® A registered trade name that may only be used by members of the NATIONAL ASSOCIATION OF REALTORS®.

Refinance: Obtaining a new loan to pay off an existing loan. Refinancing is a popular practice when interest rates drop.

REIT: Real Estate Investment Trust, a conduit entity that invests in real estate and avoids corporate taxation on distributed income. Requires emphasis on long term real estate investing and the payout of nearly all taxable income. See www.NAREIT.org for current rules and a history of REITs starting from their initial authorization in January of 1961.

Restrictive Covenants: Private restrictions limiting the use of real property. Restrictive covenants are created by deed and may "run with the land," binding all subsequent purchasers of the land, or may be "personal" and binding only between the original seller and buyer. Restrictive covenants may limit the density of buildings per acre, regulate size, style or price range of buildings to be erected.

Reversion Capitalization Rate: The overall capitalization rate used to determine the Reversion Value based on the end of year NOI or next year NOI divided by a capitalization rate.

Sales Comparison Value: A value indication derived by comparing the property being appraised to similar properties that have been sold recently, applying appropriate units of comparison, and making adjustments to the sales prices of the comparable based on the differences from the subject property. Comparables are adjusted to reflect what they would sell for if they were identical to the subject property being appraised.

Selling Agent: The agent who obtains a buyer. A selling agent may represent the buyer, or may be a subagent of the seller.

Smart Growth: "Smart growth recognizes connections between development and quality of life. In general, smart growth invests time, attention, and resources in restoring community and vitality to center cities and older suburbs. New smart growth is more town-centered, is transit and pedestrian oriented, and has a greater mix of housing, commercial and retail uses. It also preserves open space and many other environmental amenities.

Special Assessments: A special tax imposed on property, individual lots or all property in the immediate area, for road construction, sidewalks, sewers, street lights, etc.

Special Lien: A lien that binds a specified piece of property, unlike a general lien, which is levied against all one's assets. It creates a right to retain something of value belonging to another person as compensation for labor, material, or money expended in that person's behalf. In some localities it is called "particular" lien or "specific" lien. (See lien.)

Special Warranty Deed: A deed in which the grantor conveys title to the grantee and agrees to protect the grantee against title defects or claims asserted by the grantor and those persons whose right to assert a claim against the title arose during the period the grantor held title to the property. In a special warranty deed the grantor guarantees to the grantee that he has done nothing during the time he held title to the property which has impaired the grantee's title.

Speculative Property: Speculative properties are not yet leased or pre-sold. Developers are "speculating" on future real estate demand prior to or just after the completion of the building.

Stabilized Net Operating Income: Projected income less expenses that are both subject to change, but that have been adjusted to reflect equivalent, stable property operations. Unusually low occupancy or low occupancy might be viewed as temporary and atypical given rise to the use of Stabilized NOI for appraisal purposes.

Subagent: A salesperson who works for an agent.

Survey: A map or plat made by a licensed surveyor showing the results of measuring the land with its elevations, improvements, boundaries, and its relationship to surrounding tracts of land. A survey is often required by the lender to assure him that a building is actually sited on the land according to its legal description.

Sustainable Development: There are several definitions to sustainable development. Here are two: "Sustainable development meets the needs of the present without compromising the ability of future generations to meet their own needs" from the United Nations World Commission on Environment and Development.

Take-out loan: Refers to a permanent mortgage loan used to "take out" a construction loan.

Tenant Improvements or (TI): Landlord-provided improvements included in the space such as wall finish, carpeting, and lighting.

Tenant Representative or Tenant Rep: Specializes in negotiating for tenants. The tenant representatives' company should, preferably, not also be leasing agents, i.e., landlord representatives.

Title Insurance: An insurance policy that protects against losses arising from title defects such as forged or miss-filed documents. Protects lenders against loss of their interest in property due to legal defects in title.

Title Search or Examination: An examination of the public records to determine whether the current title is clear or defective.

Title: Lawful ownership of property. As generally used, the rights of ownership and possession of particular property. In real estate usage, title may refer to the instruments or documents by which a right of ownership is established (title documents), or it may refer to the ownership interest one has in the real estate.

VA (Veterans Administration): A federal agency designed to help veterans enter the housing market. A loan guaranteed by the U.S. Department of Veterans Affairs (VA). VA loans are made to honorably discharged veterans.

Walk-Through: A final inspection of a property before it changes ownership.

Zoning Ordinances: The acts of an authorized local government establishing regulations for property land usage, type of use, density, and set-backs.

NAIOP Terms and Definitions: U.S. Office and Industrial Market

The NAIOP Research Foundation funded a standardization project that would define selected office and industrial real estate terms commonly used by owners, brokers, developers and others in their day-to-day business operations. To accomplish this task, NAIOP assembled a Task Force consisting of representatives from a cross-section of NAIOP's membership including developers, investors, financiers, and brokerage and research organizations. A Project Team, spearheaded by Deloitte Consulting LLC, and also consisting of members of NAIOP's senior management and industry consultants, gathered and constructed definitions and solicited comments and recommendations from the Task Force.

Definitions for selected commonly used office and industrial terms were gathered from real estate associations, research organizations, developers and technology providers. For certain terms, existing definitions provided from these groups were incorporated as-is, with attribution. For other terms, new definitions were constructed.

The standardized terminology documents are available on the NAIOP Web site at http://www.naiop.org/foundation/completedresearch.cfm.